Are you what you eat?

DK

Penguin Random House

Senior Editors Anne Hildyard, Wendy Horobin
Senior Art Editors Clare Shedden, Hannah Moore
Project editors Ann Baggaley, Carrie Love,
James Mitchem
Senior designers Claire Patané, Sadie Thomas,
Samantha Richiardi
Designer Charlotte Bull
Design Assistant Stefan Georgiou
Senior Jacket Creative Nicola Powling

Producer, Pre-Production Tony Phipps
Producer Ché Creasey
Creative Technical Support Sonia Charbonnier

Managing Editor Penny Smith
Managing Art Editor Marianne Markham

Creative Director Jane Bull
Publisher Mary Ling

Consultant Nutritionist Fiona Hunter

First published in Great Britain in 2015
by Dorling Kindersley Limited,
80 Strand, London WC2R 0RL

A Penguin Random House Company

2 4 6 8 10 9 7 5 3 1

001–270921–April/2015
Copyright © 2015 Dorling Kindersley Limited
All rights reserved.

A CIP catalogue record for this book
is available from the British Library.

ISBN 978-0-2411-8234-5

Printed and bound in China.

A WORLD OF NEW IDEAS
SEE ALL THERE IS TO KNOW AT

www.dk.com

There is no sincerer love
than the love of food.
George Bernard Shaw (1856–1950)

Building the BODY

Which FUEL?

How much is ENOUGH?

CONTENTS

The spark of civilization

"Tell me what you eat, and I will tell you what you are".

Jean Anthelme Brillat-Savarin

What's cooking?

All living creatures need to eat, but humans are the only species that cook their food. This often overlooked difference could be one of the key reasons for the advancement of mankind. Around 2 million years ago, our ancestors had smaller brains and larger stomachs. They spent their energy foraging, chewing, and digesting whatever they could find...

...but then, man discovered fire.

After we began cooking our food, our *digestive systems became smaller and more efficient*. Our brains grew, allowing us to develop new methods to acquire our food – from creating tools and better ways to hunt, to cultivating crops and rearing animals, and eventually to creating entirely new foods.

As our *technology* and *relationship with food* has advanced, so has humanity as a species. *We can no longer survive without cooking.* Which leaves us with the question:

ARE YOU WHAT YOU EAT?

Early discoveries

After man discovered tools and fire, life became a lot easier. From then on, animals were farmed, and foods were developed that we recognize and still enjoy today, such as bread and tea.

5000 BCE
The first evidence of cheese-making was in Poland. However, cheese may have been made before this. Early man could not digest milk, but could eat cheese and other fermented dairy products.

30,000 BCE
Flour made from roots and from the plant cattails were made into an early form of flat bread.

6000 BCE
Grapes grown in the Southern Caucasus were used to make the first wine.

30,000 BCE　　**10,000 BCE**　　**5000 BCE**

10,000 BCE
Goats were domesticated across Central Asia.

Naaaaa!

7000 BCE
Cereals were grown in Syria, rice and millet in China, and maize-like plants in Mexico. Sheep were domesticated (with the help of dogs) in Western Asia.

12,000 BCE
The first grain, called Einkorn, and strains of rice were cultivated.

2700 BCE
Legend has it that the Chinese emperor Shen Nung discovered you could drink tea when plant leaves fell into a pot of boiling water.

1500 BCE
Egyptian scrolls showed the use of anise, saffron, mustard, garlic, parsley, poppy seeds, and other plants as medicines.

400 BCE
The Greek physician Hippocrates conducted studies linking food and health. He famously told his students "Let thy food be thy medicine and thy medicine be thy food." One of the earliest mentions of vinegar and its health benefits are in his works.

3000 BCE   2000 BCE   1000 BCE

3000 BCE
Palm oil was found in Egyptian tombs along with fluffy bread. This type of bread was made when wild yeast in the air caused it to rise. Tomb paintings also show fish ponds and fruit trees.

1900 BCE
Cocoa was made into a frothy but bitter chocolate drink by early Central American civilizations.

500 BCE
Sugarcane was turned into giant sugar crystals in India by boiling the stems and cooling the juice.

New discoveries

As human civilization grew, new foods such as preserved fish, pizza, and even peanut butter began to form part of people's diets. They are still popular today, as are cookbooks – the earliest written almost 2,000 years ago!

100 The approximate date of the oldest known cookbook, thought to have been written by a 1st century Roman called Apicius. He loved food so much it is thought he ate himself to death! The first mechanical dough mixer was invented. It was a stone basin with wooden paddles, powered by a donkey walking around in circles.

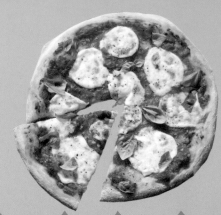

1000 The first mention of pizza was written in a document in Gaeta, Italy. Tomatoes were unknown, so the topping was often raisins and honey.

100CE   500   1000

700
An early form of sushi was invented in Southeast Asia as a means of preserving fish. The fish was salted, then coated in boiled rice and left to ferment for months. The rice was then scraped off and the fish was eaten.

I'M A CHINESE SALMON...

...AND I'M A SALTY VIKING COD

1000 Although cod was already being salted and dried by the Vikings, it became a Europe-wide phenomenon when Basque sailors discovered cod fishing grounds and worked out how to salt it at sea. A religious law that meat must not be eaten on Fridays made salt cod extremely popular, and the fish supper was born.

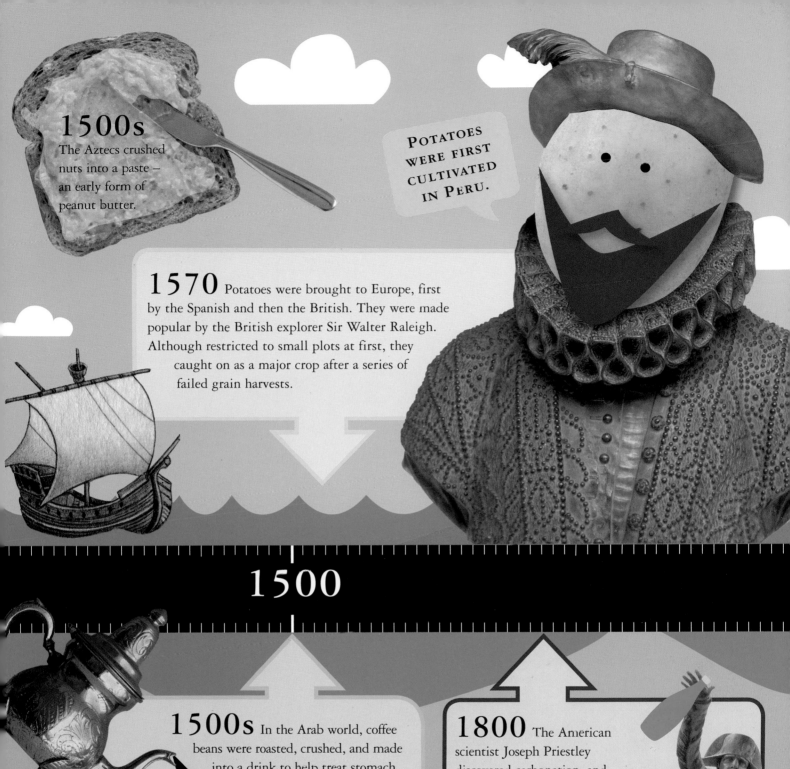

1500s
The Aztecs crushed nuts into a paste — an early form of peanut butter.

POTATOES WERE FIRST CULTIVATED IN PERU.

1570 Potatoes were brought to Europe, first by the Spanish and then the British. They were made popular by the British explorer Sir Walter Raleigh. Although restricted to small plots at first, they caught on as a major crop after a series of failed grain harvests.

1500

1500s In the Arab world, coffee beans were roasted, crushed, and made into a drink to help treat stomach aches and narcolepsy, which is a condition causing people to suddenly fall asleep. By the 16th century there were coffee houses across the Arabian Peninsula, and by the 17th century they were found across Europe.

1800 The American scientist Joseph Priestley discovered carbonation, and started a demand for fizzy water. Napoleon's need to feed his troops encouraged the development of a way to heat-seal food in bottles, which then progressed to unbreakable cans. Unfortunately the lead in some tin cans proved to be toxic. Enamel-lined tins didn't appear until 1928.

Moving forward

From the middle of the 19th century, scientists invented new ways to farm and process food. Pre-made meals and improved technology ensured a longer shelf-life, and new, famous food products were invented.

I'M NOT SURE WHAT IT IS, BUT IT LOOKS TASTY!

1885 While inspiration for the hamburger came from Hamburg, Germany, it was really perfected in the USA. The earliest mention of it was in 1885 in Texas.

1830   1850   1880

1834 British inventor James Sharp created the first gas cooker for homes, but it took several years for them to become popular.

1864 French chemist Louis Pasteur invented pasteurization, a way to preserve milk, beer, and wine.

1886 Coca-Cola® was created as a medicine in Atlanta, Georgia, by John Pemberton. The original recipe contained cocaine, which wasn't removed until 1903. Since 2013 it has been officially available in every country in the world except Cuba and North Korea. But it is available there too – unofficially.

1928 As a reaction to unsanitary conditions in many bakeries, people became afraid of possible food-borne illnesses. This led to a rise in factory-made processed foods. The first sliced loaf was packaged and sold.

1904 Tractors and new mechanical technology revolutionized the farming industry, allowing farmers to sow and harvest crops at a much higher rate.

THESE MACHINES MAKE MY LIFE EASIER.

1890   1910   1930

1910s World War I saw rationing introduced in many parts of the world. Canned food increased in popularity, and scientists worked to improve food quality and processes, to increase yields and storage, and to reduce malnutrition among the working classes.

1895 John Harvey Kellogg invented the corn flake with his younger brother Will Keith Kellogg. The story goes it was created when they let cooked wheat turn stale by accident.

1912 Polish chemist Casimir Funk discovered vitamins – a major turning point in our understanding of health and nutrition.

Modern methods

The last hundred or so years was all about convenience, as scientists invented new technology and ways to freeze, chill, and process food. However, this convenience created a rise in concern about artificial food.

1960s

Following a surge in technology, new containers including plastic cartons, aluminium cans with ring-pull tabs, foil linings, and resealable lids were invented. Freeze-dried and tubed food was used to feed the first astronauts, and on Earth, convenience food took over, with the rise of instant mashed potato, powdered soup, and freeze-dried coffee.

1930   **1940**   **1950**   **1960**

1930s SPAM®

was invented in 1937 and then given to US troops as rations in World War II. It was quickly adopted by other Allied forces and people in the countries they were stationed in. Black-market supplies were later used as unofficial currency during the Korean War.

1934

Teflon, one of the most slippery substances on Earth, was invented by accident. By the 1960s the non-stick pan had become a household item.

1950s

Clarence Birdseye's frozen foods became available for owners of the new home refrigerators.

1970s Bar codes helped manufacturers and supermarkets keep track of products, and made pricing errors much less likely.

1994 Research into GMO (genetically modified organism) crops caused alarm over their unknown consequences for health and farming.

1980s Chilled prepared food (ready meals), artificial protein (eg. Quorn), and low-calorie meals and drinks were produced.

2013 3D printing technology took off. Models were created that could print certain foods, such as chocolate and sweets, into unusual shapes.

"Cold chains" or temperature-controlled supply chains meant that fresh products could be transported from all over the world and into the shops within days.

1970   **1980**   **1990**   **2000**

1967 The first domestic microwave was sold in the US. Because of its high price tag and the fact that many people were worried about cooking with radiation, it took more than a decade before microwaves became popular.

1990s Concerns about artificial ingredients and over-processed foods started a swing back to more organic methods of farming and home-cooked food. Cookery programmes filled the airwaves, and chefs around the world became famous.

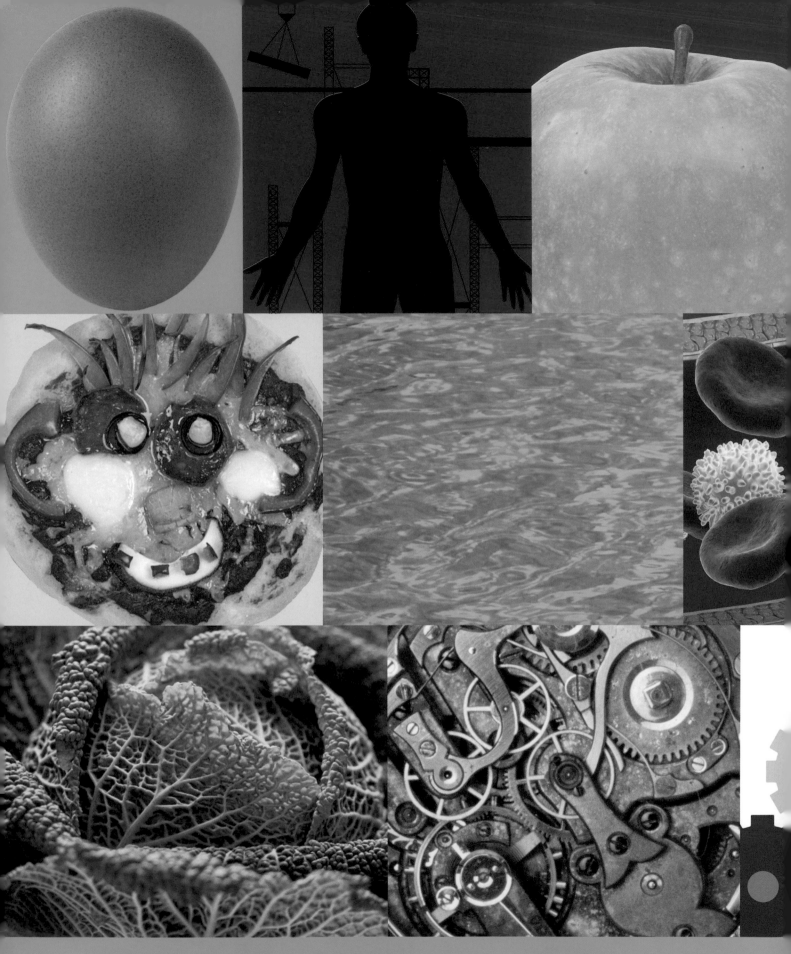

BUILDING the body

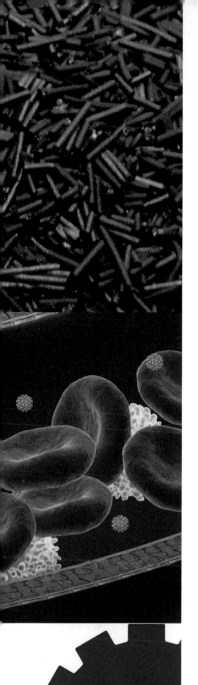

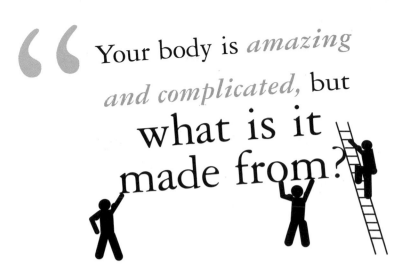

"Your body is *amazing and complicated*, but **what is it made from?**

The answer is *trillions and trillions of tiny building blocks called cells.* These cells all work together to build and maintain your bones, blood, hair, skin and all the other little bits that make you, well, you.

The *food you eat plays a vital role* in keeping your cells, and therefore your body, working properly."

My body runs like clockwork.

Recipe for a human

You really are what you eat. Like everything else in the Universe you are made of atoms of different elements. There are 92 naturally occurring elements, but it takes only 13 of them, plus traces of up to 60 others, to make a human. Here are the ingredients that make up you.

Oxygen 65%
Around two-thirds of your body is oxygen. It is usually combined with hydrogen in the form of water (it's the O in H_2O (water), but is also found in all body tissues. You renew oxygen supplies every time you breathe in or take a drink.

Carbon 18%
Carbon – the same ingredient that makes coal and diamonds – accounts for nearly a fifth of your body. It is found throughout the body because of its ability to form complex chemicals, such as those found in muscles, bones, and skin.

Hydrogen 10%
Hydrogen was the first element to form in the Universe. It has the smallest and lightest atoms of all the elements and is very reactive. In the body it is mainly found in water or combined with carbon.

Nitrogen 3%
Nitrogen is vital for making chemicals called amino acids that combine to form the proteins found in muscles, nerves, skin, and many other parts of the body.

Calcium 1.4%
This element is mainly found in the hard structures of the body, such as the bones and teeth. It also keeps the heart beating and helps the muscles to work.

Phosphorus 1.1%
Phosphorus is what makes a struck match burst into flames, but in the body it helps strengthen bones and teeth. It is also part of the membrane that surrounds cells and plays a vital role in how the body makes energy.

Potassium 0.35%
Without potassium you would not be able to move a muscle, and it helps keep body fluids in balance. This element helps nerve signals to travel around the body and also regulates the heartbeat.

Sulphur 0.25%
Sulphur is found in most of the body's soft tissues. It has an odour like rotten eggs, and is responsible for many of the body's worst smells.

Sodium 0.15%
Sodium plays a vital role in how nerves transmit signals, and also helps control the amount of water in the body.

Chlorine 0.15%
This green gas is usually combined with sodium in the body to form salt (sodium chloride). Salt is found in many body fluids, including in your tears.

What's cooking? *You!* Add 13 elements and

WHAT ELSE?
The rest of the body (0.54198%) is made up of tiny but essential pinches of other elements, including copper, zinc, fluorine, selenium, manganese, cobalt, and aluminium. You are even a little bit radioactive – some forms of potassium and carbon are *radioactive.* Uranium exists in food and water in small amounts. It is found in soil, rocks, water, and plants worldwide.

Magnesium 0.05%
Magnesium is important for the skeleton and for muscle contraction. It is also vital to the working of many enzymes.

Iron 0.008%
Iron in the blood captures oxygen breathed in through the lungs and carries it around the body to the cells that need it. You don't need much of it – there is only enough in the body to make a single iron nail.

Iodine 0.00002%
Despite the tiny quantity, iodine is essential for the production of energy by cells. Without it you would find it hard to function.

a pinch of this & that.

Building blocks

Your whole body is made up of trillions of building blocks called cells. If you could line them up end to end, they would go around the earth a few times. They are called cells because the man who first saw them under a microscope thought they looked like a monk's room, which is known as a cell.

It would take around 40 cells to fill this full stop!

THE STRUCTURE OF A CELL

For their tiny size, cells are amazing. They come in all sorts of shapes and sizes and can do hundreds of different jobs in the body, depending on how they are programmed.

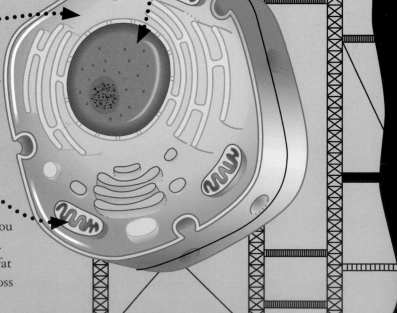

Nucleus
This controls the rest of the cell. It's where the majority of our DNA is held – this determines how we look.

Cytoplasm
The living jelly-like substance contains the nucleus and mitochondria.

Cell membrane
This is a thin skin around the cell that holds everything together and controls what goes in and out of the cell.

Mitochondria
They produce energy from nutrients that you eat, plus oxygen, to make the cell function. Most of the energy comes from glucose or fat in the diet. The molecules have to pass across a cell membrane, which is semi-permeable.

Did you know that what you eat affects

We have about 200 different types of cells in the body.

Although there are no typical cells, they all need similar elements to build them. Here are a few of the body's most important cells and what foods they need to stay healthy.

Brain cell

Fats make up 60 per cent of the brain and nervous system. So good fats help the brain to work well. One group of omega-3 fatty acids is so important, it is known as "brain food".

Omega-3 oils

Found in oil-rich fish such as fresh tuna, mackerel, and salmon, also in walnuts and linseeds.

Bone cell

Calcium is a vital mineral. It holds cells in your bones together to give them a strong foundation. It is used by the nerves and muscles, and it's needed for healthy tooth enamel.

Calcium

Milk and other dairy products are rich in the mineral calcium, which is essential to building and maintaining strong bones.

Muscle cell

Our muscle cells are made of protein. To grow strong healthy muscles, regular exercise and a well-balanced diet will fuel the muscles; protein foods help them to grow.

Protein

High quality protein foods such as eggs supply the amino acids needed for building muscle.

Blood cell

The blood cells carry oxygen around the body. This is vital to provide energy for everyday activities. To function properly they need the mineral iron.

Iron

Dark leafy greens, red meat, liver, and shellfish are rich in iron.

all the *trillions* of cells in the body?

Fuelling the body

Just as a machine needs fuel to generate power, we require fuel in the form of food to give us energy to be active, play, and grow. Our food provides nutrients in the shape of carbohydrates, fats, protein, vitamins, and minerals. These all do different jobs in the body. Proteins are used for building tissues and organs, while fats maintain body heat and carry vitamins around, and carbohydrates supply the majority of your energy.

WHAT GOES IN

You can't get by on just one type of fuel – a balance of all the right food groups will give you enough energy for all your activities.

Bread, rice, potatoes, pasta and *other starchy foods*

Vegetables

Fruits

Foods and drinks high in *fats* and *sugars*

Milk and other *dairy foods*

Meat, fish, eggs, beans, and *other proteins*

Don't forget to drink *plenty of water*, too!

Fats and sugars are important, but having too many of them can be harmful.

Dark green vegetables have substances that protect your vision.

For healthy bones, stay active, get out in the sunshine, and drink your milk! It has calcium that's good for teeth, too.

To keep things running smoothly, eat lots of wholegrain pulses, beans, and cereals.

Build up *muscles* with regular exercise

The more vegetables of all colours, the better, and don't forget fruits too.

Eat fresh fruits with the skin on for added fibre.

Go for olive oil, and avoid spreads.

Get your calcium from this group.

Protein helps to build and repair muscles.

WHICH FUEL?

Carbohydrates

These starchy foods include oats, wholegrains, rice, pasta, cereals, lentils, beans, and potatoes. They supply energy as glucose to all the cells.

Vegetables

All vegetables – fresh, frozen, and canned, contain essential vitamins and minerals. They're good for everything, including digestion, and eyesight.

Fruit

Get colourful! Fruits give you fibre and important nutrients such as vitamins and minerals. Fruits contain chemicals that protect the body's cells from harm.

Fats and sugars

Foods include butter, oils, mayonnaise, sweets, crisps, sugar, cookies, and sugary drinks. Don't eat too many of these. Try healthier options such as avocado or oily fish. These provide energy, vitamins A and D, and essential fats.

Calcium

Dairy foods such as milk, cheese, and yogurt are rich in calcium, which is needed for strong bones and teeth. They provide calcium, protein, and vitamin B12.

Protein

Foods such as meat, fish, cheese, milk, eggs, nuts, and soya beans contain protein. It's needed for growth, repair, and maintenance.

Feeling hungry

The urge to eat is partly driven by how much energy you need to keep your body functioning and how nutritious your food is. However, there are various other things that can trigger feelings of hunger.

Feed me!

When you get hungry your stomach will growl, and you will feel weak or dizzy. These signals that you need to eat are controlled by a region of the brain called the hypothalamus, which responds to hormones made by your digestive system. The hormone levels tell the brain how empty or full you are. The level of sugar in your blood also prompts the brain to tell you to eat.

Hunger hormones

The two hormones responsible for controlling your appetite are called ghrelin and leptin. Ghrelin is mainly produced by the stomach. Its levels increase rapidly when you need to eat, and decrease for a few hours after a meal. Leptin is produced by the intestines and tells the brain when your body has enough stored energy.

Eating by the clock

Our bodies have built-in rhythms that prompt us to do things like sleep and eat, but we also divide up our day with clocks. When we wake up we have breakfast, at noon it's lunchtime, and then dinner is in the evening, a few hours before we go to bed. In between, we may have various snacks. Working patterns can alter eating routines, for example, for shift workers.

When the *brain* gets an "empty" signal from *hormones* in your digestive system, it lets you know it's *time to eat.*

Growl

Hunger and cravings aren't the same. The digestive system *controls* hunger, whereas the brain is *responsible* for cravings.

AROUND 80% OF FLAVOUR COMES FROM SMELL

Sensory triggers

Feelings of hunger can also be triggered just by the sight and smell of food. The aroma of freshly baked bread or the sight of a juicy strawberry can make you feel hungry even when you're not. Sometimes you may want a particular taste such as something sweet or salty, and you will go on feeling hungry until you have satisfied this craving. Foods that you dislike don't have this effect.

Blood sugar

Energy is provided to the body's cells as glucose (sugar) dissolved in the blood. Sugar levels in our cells are controlled by a hormone called insulin created by the pancreas. They go up and down during the day, dropping before you have a meal and rising after.

Does *this look* tasty?

Rumbly tummy

Your stomach contracts at regular intervals, even when empty. The noises it makes come from trapped air that gets squashed around. The medical name for tummy rumbles is *borborygmi*.

Food blues

Does colour affect what you want to eat? If offered a red or a blue apple, most people would choose red because it is a more appetizing colour. Blue is not a natural colour for food and is mainly used in other manufactured items. Carrots were once mostly purple, but people prefer to eat orange ones as they are more appealing.

Down *the* HATCH

The food you eat is not immediately useful to your body. It first has to go on a long journey through the digestive system. On the way, it is turned into molecules small enough to be transported by your blood to all the cells of the body.

An empty stomach is about the size of a fist, *but can expand* to the size of a *football*.

1 Nose
Digestion starts when your nose detects an appetizing smell.

2 Mouth
Food is chewed and mixed with saliva, which contains amylase, a digestive enzyme. This breaks down starch into simpler sugars.

Tongue

Food being pushed towards the throat by the tongue

Saliva gland

3 Epiglottis
This is a flap at the base of the tongue that tilts when you swallow. It covers the opening to the windpipe to stop food entering.

4 Gullet or oesophagus
The tube that carries food from the back of the tongue and down the throat to the stomach. Food is moved by a series of wave-like muscle contractions, known as peristalsis.

The windpipe continues down to the lungs.

Your food takes *six to eight hours to pass* through the *stomach* and small intestine.

Tiny pits in the stomach lining produce the acid.

5 Stomach

This stretchy, muscular sack produces acid and enzymes that continue the process of breaking down the food.

7 Pancreas

This organ adds digestive juices to the small intestine. It also produces insulin and adds it to the bloodstream for the regulation of the body's glucose (sugar) level.

10 Rectum

Peristalsis moves any waste into the rectum at the end of the colon, then a signal tells the brain you need to poo.

Anus

Pyloric sphincter

Liver

Appendix

6 Gall bladder

This organ stores bile made by the liver, and adds it to the small intestine.

8 Small intestine

Nutrients are absorbed as food travels through the small intestine. They enter the bloodstream to be taken around the body.

9 Large intestine

Water and salts are absorbed from the solid food residues using bacteria that digests some of the fibre. Bacteria also help to make vitamin K and biotin.

The small intestine is covered with finger-like projections called villi. They increase the surface area of the small intestine to up to 40m² (430sq ft) – half the size of a badminton court!

Villi

THE BODY'S
chemical
LABORATORY

WATER

FOOD

SALIVA

The stomach contains
a digestive juice called
hydrochloric acid,
which is so strong
it could **dissolve**
an iron nail.

GULLET

The digestive process can be likened to an
experiment in a laboratory. The stomach
is a bit like a mixer, churning the food to
make a mushy mixture called "chyme".

A drop of this and a drop of that

Food entering the stomach starts to be broken down by digestive fluids.
An enzyme called protease begins to digest proteins with the help of the
acid in the stomach. Once reduced to soupy chyme, the food is released into
the duodenum, the first bit of the small intestine. Here, bile produced by
the liver and stored in the gallbladder is added into the small intestine to
help break down fats. At the same time, the pancreas adds alkaline juices
to neutralize the stomach acid. The watery mixture passes through the
small intestine, and nutrients are absorbed across the villi (tiny, finger-like
projections that line the small intestine), and then into the bloodstream.

Moving on

The muscular movements that churn up and move liquid food along
the small intestine are called "peristalsis". These movements are wave-like,
and keep the food moving until it reaches the large intestine.

30

The stomach lining is protected *from the acid* by mucus, *which is* made *by* *special cells in* the stomach.

STOMACH

Hydrochloric acid

PYLORIC SPHINCTER
The ring of muscle opens to let chyme into the small intestine.

PANCREAS
Digestive enzymes from the pancreas are added to the small intestine to break down food further.

LIVER
Bile is dripped into the small intestine to help in the digestion of fats.

SMALL INTESTINE

Almost 90 to 95 per cent of nutrients are absorbed in the small intestine.

Upside down
Rhythmic movements that move food through the intestine, called peristalsis, happen without you controlling them. Peristalsis also means you can eat and drink upside down. But don't put it to the test!

and then off to the large intestine, which is around 1.5m (5ft) long, and 7.6cm (3in) in diameter.

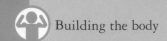

Running on *empty*

Going without *food*

How long?

Humans can only survive for a few days without water, but can go much longer without food – up to two months as long as we have enough to drink. Much depends on the temperature and whether we are doing any exercise. The more stored energy we have, the longer we can survive before our bodies start taking protein from vital organs such as the heart.

The average human, at rest, produces enough energy *as body heat* to power a LIGHT BULB *for a few minutes*.

Hibernation

Bears and other animals survive tough winters where food is scarce by putting on weight early and then going into a long sleep. During this hibernation they can lose up to 40 per cent of their body mass, but don't suffer muscle wastage or organ breakdown like humans would.

DIGESTIVE SYSTEM

Without food, the body starts to use up its energy reserves. At first it uses what is left in the digestive system.

ORGANS AND MUSCLES

After fasting for a while, protein starts to be taken from the organs and muscles. Finally, as a last resort, protein is taken from the heart muscles, and it eventually stops beating.

BRAIN

The brain needs protein and glucose to function. Without food, things such as your memory, and musc[le] movements will be affecte[d]

LIVER

After energy is used up from the digestive system, the body starts to burn glycogen, a type of glucose, which is stored in the liver and muscles. This lasts for around 24 hours. Then the body breaks down fat deposits.

MUSCLE SPASMS

In severe starvation, the body experiences symptoms that include spasms of the muscles.

If you are feeling cold, you'll use up more energy.

Humans need to eat and drink. Without food and water we would not have energy to move around and function. Water is needed by every cell, tissue, and organ in the body. Having too little water or food is a big problem – we simply can't survive without it.

Why we need *water*

SALIVA
Made of around 98 per cent water, saliva is vital for moistening food and starting off the digestive process.

BRAIN
To keep your brain working efficiently, it needs to be well hydrated. Fluids help memory and mental ability.

LUNGS
Oxygen is taken in and diffuses into the bloodstream. The air that we breathe out is saturated with water vapour. On cold days, you can see your breath condensing when you breathe out.

KIDNEYS
These vital organs filter your blood and maintain the correct balance of water in the body.

LARGE INTESTINE
Water is essential to move waste material along easily and prevent constipation.

SWEAT
This is mostly water with some salts. Sweating helps cool the body when it is hot.

Human adults are around 60 per cent water.

BLOOD
The blood carries nutrients and oxygen to the cells – plasma is made of 92 per cent water.

Body of water
Water is the most important thing for our bodies. It's in the blood, bones, and organs. We are also very leaky, losing water when we sweat, go to the toilet, and breathe out. Nearly 80 per cent of the water we need every day comes from drinking, 20 per cent comes from the food we eat, and a tiny amount is made by the body. Every cell in the body needs water so that it can work properly. Water is also vital for lubricating the joints, making saliva and digestive fluids, and letting oxygen and other chemicals pass in and out of cells.

HELP!

Too much
An excess of water is as bad for you as too little. If there's too much, the kidneys cannot process it and the blood becomes diluted. Water then rushes in to some of the cells, making them swell. In the brain, where there is no more room for cells to expand, it can be fatal, because the brain can't work properly to control vital functions such as breathing.

The human body is good at keeping its systems in balance. Water taken in is equal to that removed. However, during very hot weather or after exercise, we can lose a lot of water through sweat. This water must be replaced to avoid dehydration.

Lifetime *NUTRITIONAL* needs

At every age, a good diet is all about balance and eating a good variety of foods. But during different stages of your life, more or less of one nutrient may be needed.

> I'm not growing so fast, but I have growth spurts, so my appetite can vary.

> I'm growing fast and have high nutritional needs. I have a small stomach so need regular snacks and nutrient-rich foods. Until I'm 2, I still need full-fat milk to give me enough calories to grow.

> I should get all the nutrients I need from breast or formula milk. Around 6 months, I will start to be weaned, which means introducing some new foods into my diet.

INFANT

NUTRIENTS
Fat, protein, vitamins A, C, and D, and minerals.

WHY ARE THEY NEEDED?
To develop strong and healthy bones and muscles, and to promote the growth of healthy skin, hair, and eyes.

WHERE TO FIND KEY NUTRIENTS?
Breast or formula milk contains all the essential nutrients that are needed up until six months.

1–3 YEARS

NUTRIENTS
Calcium, iron, and zinc are key minerals at this stage, as are vitamins A, C, and D.

WHY ARE THEY NEEDED?
To develop the immune system and continue to build a healthy body with strong bones, teeth, and muscles.

WHERE TO FIND KEY NUTRIENTS?
Vitamins are found in meat, eggs, fruit. Calcium is found in vegetables. Iron and zinc are in pulses, fish, and lean meat.

4–7 YEARS

NUTRIENTS
Calcium and B vitamins, and minerals such as zinc.

WHY ARE THEY NEEDED?
Calcium is a priority for bones and teeth. B vitamins are needed to build healthy cells and a robust nervous system.

WHERE TO FIND KEY NUTRIENTS?
Milk, cheese, and yogurt contain calcium. Lean meat and green vegetables provide vitamins. Zinc is in fruit, vegetables, and fish.

> My bones are still growing, so getting a healthy diet with enough calcium and vitamin D will help my bones to grow stronger. This will protect them in later life.

> I sometimes feel a bit moody, and I've started to get spots, but if I have my fill of vitamins and minerals in fruit and vegetables things should get better. Also, my bones still need regular calcium and vitamin D.

8–11 YEARS

12–19 YEARS

NUTRIENTS
Carbohydrates, fat, protein, calcium, zinc, and vitamins A, C, E, B are vital.

WHY ARE THEY NEEDED?
B vitamins boost concentration. Calcium is needed for bones and teeth. Zinc and vitamins power the immune system.

WHERE TO FIND KEY NUTRIENTS?
A diet with meat, poultry, fish, pulses, eggs, wholegrains, and green vegetables contains the essential nutrients.

NUTRIENTS
During adolescence, calcium, iron, vitamin D, and protein are important.

WHY ARE THEY NEEDED?
Calcium and vitamin D help growing bones. Iron is needed for the blood. Protein is used for muscle growth.

WHERE TO FIND KEY NUTRIENTS?
Liver, beef, wholegrains, leafy greens, nuts, eggs, pulses, and soy products.

FAQ

Why is breakfast the most important meal of the day?

Because you use energy even when you are asleep. Eating when you get up replaces the lost energy and fires you up for the morning ahead. You'll feel more alert and have more energy throughout the day and won't be tempted to eat a sugary snack. Eggs and wholemeal toast is a good option.

Why should I eat oily fish?

They're good for your brain, and like all protein, they help repair your body and keep it in good condition. They may even reduce your risk of getting certain diseases.

How much water should I drink each day?

Try to drink eight to ten cups daily, especially when the weather is hot or you've been playing a sport or doing exercise.

What's so good about exercise?

There are so many benefits to being active including boosting energy, helping to control weight, expanding the lungs, strengthening the heart, improving sleep quality, and getting rid of waste from the body.

What should I eat before going to bed?

You shouldn't eat immediately before bed, but at dinner you could eat something high in tryptophan, an amino acid found in proteins that promotes sleepiness. Try wholegrain pasta with vegetables and a light cheese sauce.

WHICH fuel?

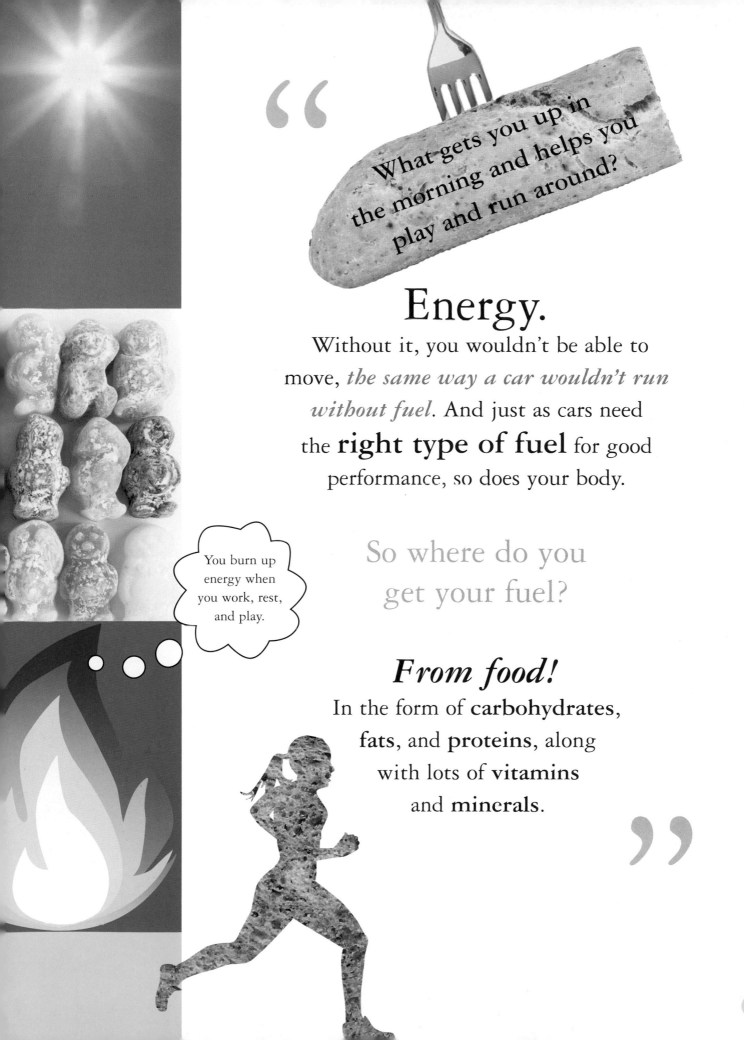

" What gets you up in the morning and helps you play and run around?

Energy.

Without it, you wouldn't be able to move, *the same way a car wouldn't run without fuel.* And just as cars need the **right type of fuel** for good performance, so does your body.

You burn up energy when you work, rest, and play.

So where do you get your fuel?

From food!

In the form of **carbohydrates**, **fats**, and **proteins**, along with lots of **vitamins** and **minerals**. *"*

What's in food?

You need nutrients in food to stay healthy. Choose foods from each food group to get a variety – and get the nutrition you need. These come in the form of carbohydrates, proteins, calcium, vitamins and minerals, and fats and sugars. What foods are they found in?

STARCHY CARBOHYDRATES

PROTEINS

FOODS THAT ARE HIGH IN CARBOHYDRATES include bread, pasta, rice, cereal, chappatis, yams, and noodles. The healthiest sources are wholegrain or minimally processed foods.

FOODS THAT ARE HIGH IN PROTEINS include meat, nuts, beans and pulses, fish, eggs, chicken, turkey, seafood, and tofu. The protein in eggs is the highest quality protein of all.

If you have a snack attack, go for *vegetable sticks, fresh fruits, unsalted nuts, or a pot of yogurt.*

FATS AND SUGARS

You need fat – but the right kind of fat. Good fats are in olive oil, nuts, oily fish, and avocados. Fats to eat in moderation are those in cheese, cream, butter, and meat. The worst fat is hydrogenated fat found in processed foods such as cakes, biscuits, and ready meals – it's bad for your health. Sugar in sweets, chocolate, cookies, and cakes tastes nice, but a little goes a long way.

DAIRY FOODS

FRUITS AND VEGETABLES

FOODS THAT PROVIDE CALCIUM are mainly dairy products such as milk, cheeses, and yogurt. They also contain vitamin A, which helps you resist infections and is essential for healthy skin and eyes.

FOOD THAT PROVIDES IMPORTANT vitamins, minerals, phytochemicals, and fibre belong to this group. You need five a day minimum – a glass of juice, and fresh, frozen, canned, or dried fruit all count, too.

Energizing Carbohydrates

The *up and down roller coaster*

Carbohydrates are essential for energy. There are lots of simple carbohydrates in cakes, biscuits, doughnuts, and sweets – it's sugar!

Sugar gives you an energy rush so that you have a lot of energy for a little while, then there's a dip, leaving you feeling hungry again. Once eaten, simple carbohydrates are changed into the simplest kind of sugar – glucose, which is absorbed into the bloodstream. Any glucose not used for energy is stored as fat!

Sugar causes a spike in blood glucose levels.

SUGAR RUSH

SUGAR RUSH

When sugar levels crash, you will have no energy, and be tempted to eat more sweet stuff.

CRASH

A cupcake will provide an instant high – but only for a short time.

Excess sugar is converted to fat!

The *smooth, steady ride*

Complex carbohydrates are broken down slowly and cause your blood sugar to rise steadily – keeping you going for longer.

Generally, unprocessed, complex carbs contain good amounts of fibre, and will slowly release glucose into the blood, keeping your energy levels balanced. These carbohydrates include wholemeal bread, oats, beans, lentils, nuts, wholewheat pasta, and vegetables. If you also eat protein with your carbs, for example, egg on wholemeal toast, you will feel fuller for longer and get through the day with plenty of energy.

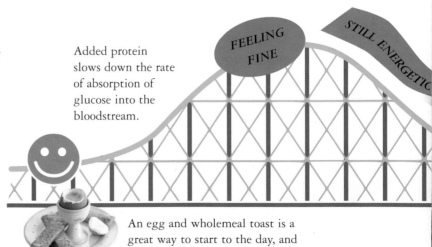

Added protein slows down the rate of absorption of glucose into the bloodstream.

FEELING FINE

STILL ENERGETIC

An egg and wholemeal toast is a great way to start to the day, and you won't be hungry until midday.

WHOLEMEAL OR WHITE BREAD?

Wholemeal bread with fibre takes a while to get digested so the blood glucose rises slowly. White bread gives a short-lived rush of energy.

Carbohydrates, or carbs, give you energy. But they're not all the same. Sugars are simple carbohydrates that release energy quickly but get used up fast, whereas starchy carbs are more complex; they release energy slowly, and it lasts longer.

Sugar rush doesn't give you energy for very long.

SUGAR RUSH

CRASH

Up and down levels are bad for your health and weight, and make you want to eat more often.

CRASH

Eat quick-release sugars *only now and again*, ideally with low-fat protein or other low-fat foods.

Sugar crashes will make you feel hungry, and can cause headaches and tiredness.

It would have been a better idea to eat something sensible!

ON TOP FORM

FEELING GOOD

That was a delicious snack!

TIME TO EAT

You won't run out of energy.

Some wholemeal bread and peanut butter will top up your energy.

Wholemeal pasta or a potato with half-fat cheese will give you lots of energy.

Carbohydrates *are the body's main* source of *energy*. They are the best *fuel source when you are* exercising or *playing a sport*.

Perfect proteins

You might know that protein is your body builder, and is very important when you're growing. Made from something called amino acids, protein is the most widespread nutrient in the body, and is a vital element of every cell.

The sequence of the amino acids in the

FAQ

What are the best proteins?
Meat such as beef is high in protein, but can contain high levels of saturated fats. Fish, turkey, chicken, beans, and lentils are good sources of lean protein.

Why are eggs so good for me?
Eggs contain high-quality protein and are full of vitamins and minerals. Also, they aren't high in unhealthy fats!

What would happen if I didn't eat enough protein?
Since your cells are made of protein, you would have fewer of them which could cause various problems with your growth and development.

WHAT DOES PROTEIN DO?

Protein is a vital nutrient because your muscles, organs, immune system and cells are all mainly made from it. You need protein for your heart to work, to breathe, walk and run, to protect you from illnesses, and provide energy. The enzymes essential to your digestion are also made of protein!

EGGS are a *high-quality* source of PROTEIN, and are great for *building muscles.*

Every cell uses protein, and

Proteins are made of chains of different amino acids.

AMINO ACIDS

A protein is a long chain of tiny building blocks (molecules) called amino acids. When you eat protein, these chains get broken down into smaller chains and are reused to make new proteins. The other way to get amino acids is by eating certain foods. However, not all foods that contain protein have all the essential amino acids you need, so various foods must be combined in order to get the right mix.

There are *20 essential amino acids.* Your body can **MAKE** *11 of them*, and you need to get the other 9 from *food.*

chain *determines* *the type of* protein.

COMPLETE PROTEINS

Complete protein sources contain all 9 of the essential amino acids our bodies can't make in the correct amounts. This is what makes them complete. Mainly animal-based, they are found in meat, fish, eggs, and dairy foods, but plant sources, such as quinoa and soy beans have all the necessary amino acids too.

Soy beans and soy products contain all the essential amino acids.

Some insects are very good sources of protein!

INCOMPLETE PROTEINS

Beans, lentils, nuts, and seeds are good sources of protein, but don't contain all the essential amino acids you need. However, you can mix and match two incomplete proteins such as corn and beans to make a complete protein. You don't even have to eat these complementary proteins at the same time, as long as they are included in your day's meals.

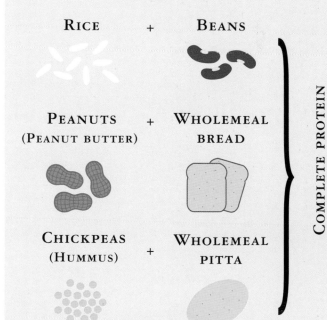

RICE + BEANS

PEANUTS (PEANUT BUTTER) + WHOLEMEAL BREAD

CHICKPEAS (HUMMUS) + WHOLEMEAL PITTA

COMPLETE PROTEIN

around 20% of the body *is made* from it.

Essential FATS

Monounsaturated fats are in avocado, peanut, rapeseed, and olive oils. Oils such as corn, sunflower and soybean oils are polyunsaturated fats.

The word "fat" sounds like a bad thing, but if you eat small amounts of the right kind, it does lots of useful jobs, such as helping your brain to develop. Fats keep you warm, give you energy, and protect your organs. But, if you eat too much, some will be stored in your body, and you'll put on weight.

FIGURE OUT FATS

There are three types: unsaturated, saturated, and trans fats. Unsaturated fats can be monounsaturated or polyunsaturated. Two types of polyunsaturates are omega-3 and 6.

UNsaturated fats

Saturated fats

Unsaturated fats are liquid at room temperature. Monounsaturated fats are found in oils such as olive oil. Polyunsaturated fats are in most vegetable oils. Omega-3 fats are found in oily fish such as fresh tuna, salmon, and mackerel. They are really good for you.

Saturated fats are usually solid at room temperature. They're found in meats and dairy products such as butter, cheese and milk, and in palm and coconut oil, which are liquids. Saturated fats are fine in small amounts.

Fat is your friend, it's great for your *skin* and *hair*, but as with your friends, **choose** the *right ones!*

Trans fats are created by adding hydrogen atoms to vegetable oils to make a solid fat. Trans fats are used by food manufacturers because they are cheap, and lengthen a food's shelf life.

Trans fats

Trans fats are in junk foods such as crisps, pies, cookies, cakes, fried foods, and doughnuts. Some margarines also contain trans fats. Trans fats are similar to saturated fat. Some studies suggest they are worse than saturated fat.

FAQ

What do fats do for you?
The monounsaturated fats in the superfood avocado, for example, help to keep your skin healthy. Pumpkin seeds make a good snack at any time, as they contain nutrients such as antioxidants and minerals. And oily fish can give a bit of a boost to your IQ!

Is there a link with sleep?
No, but lack of sleep may affect the hormone level, ghrelin, that tells us when we are hungry. This could encourage people to eat more than they should.

Where is fat stored?
Fat cells are found between the skin and muscles, and around the organs, particularly in the abdominal cavity. Fat cells are broken down into glucose and used for energy.

How can I avoid bad fats?
Have fatty fast food or junk food only occasionally, and cut back on snacks such as cakes, sweets, ice cream, doughnuts, cookies, and crisps. Instead have low-fat frozen yogurt, low-fat milk, and cheese.

Which fat is best for me?
Monounsaturates are best, then, polyunsaturated oils, then limited amounts of saturated fats in meat, cheese, and other dairy foods. Try to avoid trans fats if you can.

VITAMIN FACTS

Vitamin supplements

You only need small amounts of vitamins. If you have a varied diet you should get all the vitamins you need from food, and won't need supplements. One exception is vitamin D, which you can get from both food and the sun's rays. People who don't get enough sunlight may lack vitamin D.

Naming vitamins

Although vitamins have chemical names, they are sometimes referred to by a letter of the alphabet, for example, thiamine is B_1, since it was the first "B" vitamin to be discovered. Some are named after their function, such as vitamin K ("koagulazion" (clotting) in Danish).

Limeys

In the 17th century, before vitamins were discovered, sailors didn't get much fresh fruit because they spent years at sea on long voyages. As a result, many developed a skin disease called "scurvy". When it was found that vitamin C, present in limes and lemons, prevented scurvy, sailors from Britain began to eat lots of them and became known as "limeys".

Vital vitamins

Vitamins are substances found in food that help to make your body grow and develop properly. There are several different types, and each one has its own special job to do in the body. Some foods have more vitamins than others, and different foods contain different vitamins, so eating a varied diet is the best way to make sure you get all the vitamins you need.

Mackerel and salmon are good sources of B vitamins and also vitamin D.

Vitamin K *helps to* produce blood-clotting *proteins* that prevent excessive bleeding.

There are 13 *known vitamins*. Many more

Wholegrains, nuts, oily fish, and meat are high in group B vitamins.

Citrus fruits and berries contain lots of vitamin C.

TYPES OF VITAMIN

There are two types of vitamins: fat-soluble and water-soluble. Vitamins such as A, D, E and K dissolve in fat and can be stored in the fatty tissues of your body and the liver until you need them. Water-soluble vitamins are not stored in the body and must be replaced each day because we need a continuous supply of them. If your body doesn't use them, any left over leave the body in urine.

Fresh vegetables and fruit **are the best source of *vitamins*.**

Water-soluble vitamins such as the B-complex vitamins and vitamin C can't be stored in the body. They dissolve in water, and can also be drawn out and lost during preparation or cooking.

QUIZ

1 **Which of these foods contains the highest amount of vitamin C?**
A) Red pepper
B) Lime
C) Avocado

2 **Which vitamin can you get from exposure to sunlight?**
A) Vitamin D
B) Vitamin C
C) Vitamin K

3 **"Vitamin" is a combination of which two words?**
A) Virtual amenities
B) Vitally amiable
C) Vital amine

4 **Which of the following is not a real vitamin?**
A) Vitamin A
B) Vitamin B_6
C) Vitamin Z

5 **How many known vitamins are there?**
A) 11
B) 13
C) 20

vitamin-like substances may still be *discovered*.

VITAMIN *chart*

Vitamin	What it does		Where to find it

A

RETINOL

Essential for skin, hair, eyesight, bones, and teeth. Helps in cell reproduction, and strengthens the immune system. Beta-carotene from plants is converted to vitamin A in the body.
FAT SOLUBLE

Milk, cheese, yogurt, soy milk, carrots, spinach, green peas, sweet potatoes, pumpkins, sunflower seeds, egg yolks, broccoli, liver, mango, watermelon, and tomato juice.

C

ASCORBIC ACID

A powerful antioxidant that helps protect the cells in your body from harmful free radicals. It also helps skin wounds to heal.
WATER SOLUBLE

Citrus fruits (oranges, limes, lemons, and grapefruits), melons, tomatoes, potatoes, green peppers, and leafy green vegetables.

D

CHOLECALCIFEROL

When exposed to sunlight, the body makes its own vitamin D in the skin. Vitamin D helps to absorb calcium and phosphorus, and strengthens bones and teeth.
FAT SOLUBLE

Ten minutes in the sun, three times a week, will provide 80% of the vitamin D needed. Vitamin D is also in liver, oily fish, and egg yolks.

E

TOCOPHEROL

An antioxidant that protects the cells from harmful free radicals, it is also needed for healthy skin, heart function, and the immune system.
FAT SOLUBLE

Nuts and seeds, vegetable oils, peanut butter, almonds, dairy products, wheatgerm, wholegrains, and cereals with added vitamins.

K

PHYLLOQUINONE

Needed for strong, healthy bones, and to control blood clotting, which helps wounds to heal quicker.
FAT SOLUBLE

Broccoli, Brussels sprouts, cabbage, leafy green vegetables, and olive oil. Also, friendly bacteria in your gut can provide small amounts of the vitamin.

You *can make your own vitamin D* and

Your body can't make vitamin K without the friendly bacteria in your digestive system!

Vitamin C *and vitamin E* double up as antioxidants, which can neutralize *dangerous free radicals.*

Vitamin	What it does

B

VITAMIN B COMPLEX

Although the B vitamins are chemically different from each other, they are all equally important, and they are often found in the same foods. So why are they so vital? It's because they affect metabolism, which is simply a lot of chemical reactions that take place in your cells. Your metabolism is how your body gets all the energy it needs from the food you eat.

WATER SOLUBLE

B_1

THIAMINE
Needed for growth and energy production. It also helps the function of the nervous system, muscles, heart, and digestion.

FOUND IN
Meat, fish, poultry, beans, nuts and seeds, brown rice, wholegrains, wheatgerm, and molasses.

B_2

RIBOFLAVINE
Aids growth, and helps skin, hair, and nails to grow. Prevents sores of the mouth and lips. Helps to release energy from carbohydrates.

FOUND IN
Eggs, milk, cheese, yogurt, fish, mushrooms, almonds, pork, chicken, kidney, and wheatgerm.

B_3

NIACIN
Helps to release energy from carbohydrates, and helps the digestive and nervous systems to work well.

FOUND IN
Pork, turkey, chicken, veal, lamb, salmon, swordfish, tuna, peanuts, and sunflower seeds.

B_5

PANTOTHENIC ACID
This vitamin is used to change your food into energy and to make cell membranes. It also helps to make vitamin B_{12}.

FOUND IN
Most plant and animal foods, especially nuts, lean pork, oily fish, avocados, wholegrains, and yogurt.

B_6

PYRIDOXINE
This vitamin is needed for the nervous and immune systems, and to fight infection. It also helps you digest proteins.

FOUND IN
Tuna, salmon, liver, offal, eggs, chicken, chickpeas, bananas, and potatoes.

B_7

BIOTIN
An essential vitamin for producing fatty acids that protect the skin from damage and dryness, keeping it smooth and soft.

FOUND IN
Egg yolks, liver, almonds, walnuts, carrots, cows' milk, and goats' milk.

B_9

FOLIC ACID (FOLATE)
Helps to produce and maintain healthy red blood cells. It can also help babies to grow properly inside their mum.

FOUND IN
Liver, pulses, wholegrains, bread and cereals, leafy greens, and broccoli.

B_{12}

CYANOCOBALAMIN
Needed for energy production; also helps the function of the nervous system, muscles, heart, and the digestive system.

FOUND IN
Meat such as beef, lamb, pork, offal, seafood, eggs, and dairy produce.

vitamin K; *the others all come from food.*

Eat your *minerals*

Minerals are chemicals that are found in the
Earth's crust and in rocks. Plants that grow in
the soil absorb these minerals through their
roots. Animals eat the plants. You eat the
plants, or the animals, and in this
way, absorb the minerals.

Dark green,
leafy veg
contain iron
and calcium.

Just like vitamins, minerals
are vital for your health: they
make up some of your body's
structure and regulate many
processes. If you have a balanced,
varied diet with lots of fresh fruit,
vegetables, meat, beans, and dairy
products or other calcium-rich foods,
you should get enough minerals to
help you grow and be healthy.

Sodium, chloride, and
potassium keep the
balance of water in your
blood and tissues stable.

CHLORIDE

POTASSIUM

SODIUM

CALCIUM

PHOSPHORUS

SULPHUR

MAGNESIUM

Sulphur is needed to
maintain healthy skin.

Calcium, magnesium,
and phosphorus help
to build strong,
healthy bones.

Phosphorus,
potassium, and
magnesium are
in wholemeal
bread.

MACROMINERALS

Macro means large. You need a
good amount of these minerals.

Minerals have *been found to exist*

Cheese is rich in calcium, zinc, and phosphorus.

Brazil nuts are an excellent source of the mineral selenium.

Nuts provide a mix of minerals such as iron, calcium, and zinc.

Copper helps to make enzymes.

Zinc helps you fight off infection, and is found in all the cells. It also helps your sense of taste.

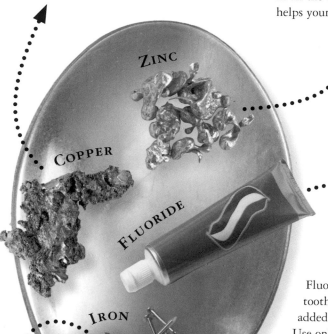

ZINC

COPPER

FLUORIDE

IRON

Iron carries oxygen around the body.

Fluoride prevents tooth decay, so it is added to toothpaste. Use only a tiny amount, and don't swallow it – it can cause side effects.

TRACE ELEMENTS

These minerals are so powerful, you only need a tiny bit of each. However, they are necessary to keep you in good health.

in all of the food groups.

DID YOU KNOW?

Mad Hatter

Some minerals aren't needed by the body and may be poisonous. In the book *Alice in Wonderland*, the Mad Hatter is thought to have behaved in a crazy way because he'd been poisoned by the mineral mercury, which was used in hat-making.

Drink up

If you eat something really salty, the sodium level in your blood increases. Water is then taken from your cells to dilute the sodium and keep the balance right. Because they've lost some of their water, the cells become dry or dehydrated, so they transmit an emergency message to the brain, which sends you a signal to have a drink of water.

Keep a balance

While you are growing, milk is good for you because it contains the calcium you need for bone growth. If, instead, you drink fizzy drinks that contain lots of phosphorus, this can upset the calcium/phosphorus balance and cause mineral deficiencies.

Iron man

There is enough iron in your body to make a nail around 7.6cm (3in) long.

MAJOR *minerals*

MACROMINERALS

Nutrients called minerals are in every bit of your body. You get them from your food, and need some of all of them to keep you fit and well.

Refreshing coconut water contains more potassium than bananas, as well as sodium, calcium, and magnesium.

Ca

CALCIUM
Helps create strong, healthy bones and teeth; helps muscles relax and contract.

FOUND IN
Milk, cheese, dairy products; canned fish eaten with their bones, legumes, kale, tofu.

Cl

CHLORIDE
Needed for fluid balance, and acid/alkali balance. Avoid too much salt; check food labels.

FOUND IN
All foods, including olives, lettuce, and salt. Large amounts in processed foods.

Mg

MAGNESIUM
Found in bones; needed for making protein, muscle contractions, nerves, and for a healthy immune system.

FOUND IN
Wholegrains, nuts and seeds, beans, and green vegetables.

P

PHOSPHORUS
Good for healthy bones and teeth; found in every cell.

FOUND IN
Meat, fish, poultry, eggs, milk, nuts, beans, seeds, dried fruits, wholemeal bread, and rice.

K

POTASSIUM
Needed for proper fluid balance, nerve transmission, and muscle contraction.

FOUND IN
Avocados, bananas, orange juice, sweet potatoes, beans, dates, and fish.

Na

SODIUM
Needed for proper fluid balance, and the working of nerves and muscles.

FOUND IN
Found in salt and in most foods. Too much can cause high blood pressure and heart disease.

S

SULPHUR
Needed for healthy skin, nails, and hair.

FOUND IN
Occurs in foods as part of protein: eggs, legumes, meat, fish, cheese, milk, and nuts.

TRACE MINERALS

Although these are present in the body in tiny amounts, they do many vital jobs in the body, including using nutrients, and making hormones.

Cr

CHROMIUM
With insulin, regulates blood sugar (glucose) levels.

FOUND IN
Beef, ham, chicken, calf's liver, wholegrains, processed meats, shellfish, apples, and bananas.

Cu

COPPER
Helps to make a protein in the blood that takes oxygen around the body. Needed for healthy cell membranes.

FOUND IN
Oysters, Brazil nuts, dried beans, dark leafy greens, beef liver, and prunes.

F

FLUORIDE
Formation of bones and teeth; helps prevent tooth decay

FOUND IN
Drinking water, seafood, including salmon, haddock, and shrimp, and teas. There are small amounts in kidney beans, lettuce, and spinach.

I

IODINE
Found in thyroid hormone, which regulates growth, development, and metabolism.

FOUND IN
Seafood, foods grown in iodine-rich soil, iodized salt, and bread.

Fe

IRON
Found in red blood cells that carry oxygen around the body. Iron is needed for energy metabolism in the body's cells.

FOUND IN
Clams, liver, and oysters, red meats, offal, egg yolks, beans, lentils, seeds, dried fruits, leafy greens, and nuts.

Mn

MANGANESE
Helps to regulate blood sugar, and convert food into energy. Essential for healthy nerves and brain.

FOUND IN
Nuts, wholegrains, dried fruits, green leafy vegetables. Sweet potatoes, lentils, and pineapple are also quite high in the mineral.

Mo

MOLYBDENUM
Triggers enzymes for many vital functions.

FOUND IN
Meats, calf's liver, legumes, grains, leafy greens, oatmeal, and green vegetables.

Se

SELENIUM
Used for antioxidants, to prevent cell damage.

FOUND IN
Brazil nuts, liver, beef, grains, mushrooms, and vegetables. Selenium levels in soil make a difference to the amount of mineral in plants and meat.

Zn

ZINC
It is needed to make around 200 enzymes, protects the immune system, and it's essential for taste perception.

FOUND IN
Meat, shellfish, milk, wholegrains, herring, and pumpkin seeds.

QUIZ

1 Which food is a good source of selenium?

A) Apricots

B) Brazil nuts

C) Seafood

2 Which is not a trace mineral?

A) Magnesium

B) Manganese

C) Molybdenum

3 Which fruit is the best source of the mineral potassium?

A) Oranges

B) Bananas

C) Apples

4 Which mineral is in toothpaste?

A) Phosphorus

B) Chloride

C) Fluoride

5 Which food is a good source of calcium?

A) Potatoes

B) Cheese

C) Pears

FIBRE IN FOOD

The amount of fibre you need varies for each person, but it's important to get enough. Remember, some foods that are healthy in other ways contain no fibre at all, so look out for these:

 1 serving popcorn
= 2½ grams of fibre

 1 apple with skin
= 4 grams of fibre

 45g (½ cup) oatmeal
= 4 grams of fibre

 75g (½ cup) frozen peas
= 4 grams of fibre

 95g (½ cup) brown rice
= 4 grams of fibre

 1 banana
= 2 grams of fibre

 1 slice wholemeal bread
= 2 grams of fibre

 1 slice white bread
= 1½ grams of fibre

 75g (½ cup) white rice
= 1 gram of fibre

 1 chicken leg
= 0 grams of fibre

 1 serving yogurt
= 0 grams of fibre

Fabulous fibre

WHICH FOODS HAVE FIBRE?

You are probably already eating fibre. Much of it comes from the skin and seeds of vegetables and fruit. If you have some of these every day – whether fresh, frozen, or canned – you should manage to get enough fibre to stay healthy. Which other foods have lots of fibre? There's plenty to choose from, including wholegrain cereals, wholemeal bread and pasta, potatoes, brown rice, beans, pulses, and nuts.

Fibre helps your digestion, and *regulates glucose in the blood,* keeping **energy levels steady.**

Research shows that kids who eat a breakfast containing wholegrains, fibre, and protein have better concentration and memory, and don't stay home from school much!

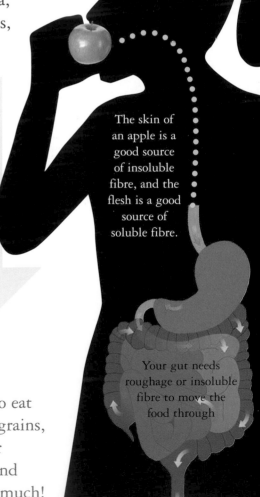

The skin of an apple is a good source of insoluble fibre, and the flesh is a good source of soluble fibre.

Your gut needs roughage or insoluble fibre to move the food through

A *western world* diet 100 years *ago*

Fibre is a carbohydrate that passes through your system undigested, helping to keep food moving smoothly through your body. This is good for your digestive organs and can prevent problems.

THE TWO TYPES OF FIBRE

Soluble

This fibre dissolves in water. It's found in beans, oat bran, carrots, oranges, and apples. This fibre slows down your digestion, so you feel full for longer. It also helps to lower fat in the blood and can slow the rate that sugar enters the bloodstream after eating, so it helps to control diabetes (too much sugar in the blood).

...and insoluble

Insoluble fibre doesn't dissolve in water. It is found in foods such as wheat, corn, and vegetables. This fibre absorbs water as it goes through the digestive system, adding bulk to the waste in your gut and speeding the process of pushing it out of your body.

We need *both* types of *fibre to keep the heart* and gut healthy.

What happens if you don't eat enough fibre?

A lack of fibre can cause you to become constipated. This is caused by food waste passing through the digestive system too slowly. The waste becomes dry and hard, and it may be difficult to go to the toilet. Drinking lots of water can help with this problem.

FAQ

High fibre foods make me fart, what can I do?

You could change your diet by cutting down on beans and fatty food. Drinking lots of water may help, and try not to swallow lots of air if you chew gum.

What are farts made of, and where do they come from?

They're gas from the intestines, which is made up of air we swallow, gas that enters the intestines from the blood, and gas produced by the chemical reactions in the gut.

What is the gas?

Hydrogen sulphide (which has a smell like rotten eggs), and smelly substances called indole and skatole. Did you know that small amounts of these are added to some perfumes!

How many times do kids fart each day?

It varies, but on average, around 14 times a day.

Why do beans make you fart?

Beans contain certain sugars that we cannot digest. These sugars react with bacteria in the large intestine to make a rich, gassy mixture, rather like dough rising when making bread. But don't worry, it is perfectly normal and healthy to have gas after eating fibre.

was **10 times** higher in **fibre** than it is **today!**

BRAIN FOODS

Avocado

Oleic acid, the fatty acid in avocados, is used to build a myelin coating in the brain, helping information to travel quickly.

Eggs

These contain cholesterol, which is needed for brain function. Eggs also contain an omega-3 fatty acid that helps form connections between brain cells.

Spinach

A good source of folate, one of the B vitamins that helps protect the brain neurons. Folate also helps to maintain healthy brain circulation.

Red meat

Meat contains iron which helps to make neurotransmitters that affect mood and brain function.

Sweet potato

The deep orange colour of sweet potatoes is caused by antioxidants called carotenoids. The body turns these into vitamin A, which is used to make nerve cells in the brain.

Brain food

Your brain is made mostly from fat and runs on carbohydrates. Like the rest of your body, it needs good nutrients such as protein, fats, and vitamins. Essential fats are vital to help brain cell production. Power up your memory, focus, and mood with these brain-boosting foods.

Oily fish

These contain essential fats that help to improve memory and the ability to learn.

Dark-green vegetables

The vitamins and antioxidants found in vegetables help to keep your brain sharp and healthy.

I'm good for your brain, so eat your greens!

Wholemeal bread

Wholegrains give the brain a slow, steady release of energy that helps keep it active.

Soak up some *sunshine,* YOUR BRAIN **needs** *vitamin* D!

Walnuts look a little like brains, too!

Walnuts

Packed with omega-3 fatty acids – an essential fat – walnuts are one of the ultimate brain foods.

Your brain is 2% of the BODY'S WEIGHT – *yet uses* 20% of its energy.

Eat a *rainbow*

Go for colour! Make sure you eat your greens, reds, whites, purples, and oranges, because many coloured fruits and vegetables contain key chemicals called phytochemicals. These help us to fight off disease, strengthen the immune system, and keep us in good working order.

High five! *Get healthy foods into your* diet with

FOOD COLOURS

White vegetables, such as cauliflower, onions, and garlic contain phytochemicals (see right) that protect your body and fight against bacteria, viruses, and cancer.

Red fruits such as apples and strawberries are rich in antioxidants. Tomatoes are a source of lycopene, which fights off disease.

Orange pumpkins, carrots, and of course, oranges are super foods for the eyes. They contain carotenes, which are converted to vitamin A, which is essential to maintain good, clear vision.

Green vegetables and fruits have powerful antioxidant properties that can help you stay sharp. They include broccoli, kale and spinach, beans, cucumber, peas, asparagus, and kiwi fruits.

Purple foods such as blackberries, blueberries, purple grapes, plums, aubergine, beetroot, and raisins contain a chemical that can protect the body from disease.

rainbow fruit and vegetables.

PLANT CHEMICALS

Natural chemical compounds found in plants, which have a protective effect on human health, are called "phytochemicals". "Phyto" refers to the Greek word for plant — all plants contain some of these compounds. There are thousands of them, but only around 100 have been identified. Although they are not essential, they are beneficial for human health.

Phytochemicals in fruits, vegetables, and other plant-based foods, protect our body in many different ways and help reduce the risk of disease.

Unlike vitamins, phytochemicals are not destroyed by chopping, grating, or cooking. In fact, sometimes the opposite is the case; the lycopene in tomatoes actually becomes more concentrated when it is processed and made into foods such as soup or sauce.

Research shows that people who eat a lot of fruits and vegetables are less likely to develop certain diseases.

ANTIOXIDANTS

Phytochemicals act as antioxidants in the body. This means that they will attack molecules (free radicals) that damage the cells.

Free radicals can enter and attack our bodies from the air, pollution, food, and drugs.

Although oxygen is essential for life, when we breathe in, oxidation occurs, and free radical bullies attack normal cells. Amazing antioxidants defend them.

Eating a variety of rainbow-coloured fruits and vegetables will provide an army of antioxidants to move around in your bloodstream, hunting down free radicals, and making them harmless. Antioxidants are more concentrated in deeply coloured fruits and dark green vegetables.

TO COOK or

Ever since our ancestors discovered how to master fire and cook food, human life changed for ever. The brain grew as early man ate more protein, laying the foundation for us to become the intelligent species we are today. But, although we know that vegetables are hugely beneficial, the question is, should we cook them or eat them raw?

THE UPSIDE

Heat can help to make some nutrients more available, but no single cooking method works for all – it's on a case by case basis.

- Cooking a vegetable, even for a very short time, makes it much easier to chew and digest.

- Cooking tomatoes breaks down tough cell walls and releases a useful phytochemical called lycopene. There's lots of it in ketchup, but the body can't get at it in raw tomatoes.

- The body can't absorb antioxidants, called carotenoids, from raw vegetables such as carrots, pumpkin, sweet potato, or peppers. The carotenoids are not available until the vegetables are cooked.

- Cooked food makes it easier for the body to digest and absorb nutrients.

- Cooking can kill germs and harmful chemicals.

THE DOWNSIDE

In some cases, heat can break down cells, causing nutrients to be lost.

- Boiling vegetables for too long can leach out nutrients such as vitamin C and B vitamins into the cooking water. This is usually then thrown away, together with the vitamins.

- Spinach loses about two-thirds of its vitamin C if cooked.

- Some antioxidants are reduced in strength after cooking.

- Vegetables can lose their vibrant colour if they are boiled.

NOT to COOK?

Why we cook meat and *fish*

Studies show that if we ate only raw food, we would have to spend an astonishing 9 hours every day eating to have enough energy to keep our brain and body working properly. This is why we need to cook most of our food. As well as getting rid of bacteria, cooking meat, fish, and poultry improves texture and taste. Less energy is used digesting it, and nutrients are absorbed quicker.

RAW FOOD

● Taking time to chew raw vegetables well breaks them down and helps digestion. The food is also absorbed more easily in the gut.

● Eating fresh, raw tomatoes gives you lots of vitamin C, but you don't get as much of their useful phytochemical lycopene if they aren't cooked.

● Broccoli may be better eaten raw; cooking it damages a useful enzyme in the vegetable that is involved in protecting the body from diseases.

COOKING METHODS MATTER

Boiling
For vegetables such as corn or courgettes, boiling helps to make it easier to absorb useful antioxidants. However, other vegetables can lose a lot of vitamin C if they are boiled.

Frying
This is the worst cooking method for retaining nutrients in vegetables, especially deep-frying. This can produce free radicals that harm body cells. Stir-frying preserves vitamins, and added fat enhances absorption.

Microwaving
This method of cooking preserves 90 per cent of vitamin C in vegetables, but can sometimes alter the texture of the food.

Steaming
Vegetables that are steamed maintain their vitamin compounds much more than if they are boiled.

Are you *really* what you EAT?

If you really are what you eat, which person would you choose to look like: the one on this page made of healthy fruits, vegetables, lean meat, and wholegrains, or the other one, made of sweet and fatty foods?

DID YOU KNOW?

The first country to develop the art of making noodles was China, before 200 BCE. Poets likened their texture to silk!

Most people find that eating asparagus gives their urine a very strong odour. It's due to a sulphur-containing substance, which is chemically close to the essence of skunk!

Research studies have found that eating wholegrains and legumes (beans, peas, and nuts), provides us with hundreds, if not thousands, of phytochemicals that can help our health.

Peanuts grow below ground and are legumes or beans, not nuts.

Avocado has the *highest protein and oil content* of all fruits. Also, the oil is the healthier, unsaturated type.

Peanuts are one of the ingredients in *dynamite!* The connection is glycerol, which is found in peanuts – nitroglycerin is the main element in dynamite.

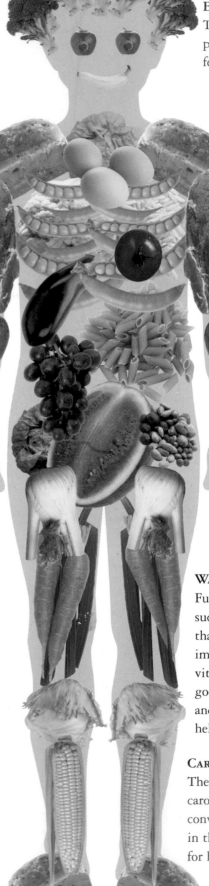

BROCCOLI
This green veg is packed with folic acid for healthy blood cells.

LEAN BEEF
Rich in protein, low in fat, it's important for body building and repair.

TOMATOES
As well as tasting good, they are a source of vitamin C and fibre.

APPLES
Full of health benefits, they are fat-free, low in calories, and provide vitamins C and A.

FENNEL
Fresh bulbs have high levels of an essential oil, anethole, thought to have anti-fungal and anti-bacterial properties.

WATERMELON
Full of nutrients such as vitamin C, that help your immune system, vitamin A, which is good for your eyesight, and vitamin B6, which helps fight infections.

WHOLEMEAL BREAD
A good source of energy, it also contains vitamin B, fibre, and iron.

CARROTS
They contain beta carotene, which is converted to vitamin A in the body. It is needed for healthy eyes.

THE 80:20 RULE

You don't need to stop eating your favourite treats, just make sure that you eat a healthy, balanced diet for about 80 per cent of the time – then indulge a little for the other 20 per cent.

DOUGHNUTS
Full of sugar, any excess is stored as fat.

POTATOES
A good source of energy and vitamin C, but are less healthy when they're coated in fat.

SWEETS
Too much of these can cause tooth decay.

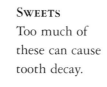

Tooth decay, heart disease, and obesity can result from too much unhealthy food.

FAQ

Why do I feel sleepy after eating spaghetti bolognese?
The meat in the sauce is protein that contains tryptophan, and it's a snooze food. Pasta is a carbohydrate, and carbs make tryptophan more available to the brain, causing your drowsiness.

How many doughnuts are eaten each year?
Statistics for the US indicate that they get through quite a few – 10 billion every year!

What are trans fats?
These are artificially-produced fats that are really bad for your health and should be avoided whenever possible. Check food labels and make sure they are not listed. Avoid foods that list ingredients such as hydrogenated oils – they are trans fats. They are often included in baked goods such as biscuits and cakes.

QUICK QUIZ

1 **Which vitamin is good for your eyesight?**

A) Vitamin B$_{12}$

B) Vitamin A

C) Vitamin C

D) Vitamin K

2 **Which vegetable has anti-bacterial properties?**

A) Celery

B) Fennel

C) Broccoli

D) Carrots

ALLERGY ADVICE

Hidden dangers

It might seem easy to avoid eating food you know makes you ill – as everyone knows what a peanut looks like. But that peanut could be somewhere unexpected – ground up, or made into oil, for example. If nuts are included as an ingredient in processed foods, a warning must be clearly stated on the label. The following are just some of the foods that may contain hidden nuts.

Cakes and biscuits

Ice cream

Breakfast cereals

Living with allergies

For anyone with a serious food allergy, here are a few ways to protect yourself from allergic reactions:

• Tell all your friends and classmates, why you can't eat some foods.

• If someone offers you food you're unsure of, say "NO THANKS".

• Never, ever risk "just one bite".

• If doctors prescribe anti-allergy medicines, make sure to carry them with you.

• Wear a medic alert bracelet. If you are taken ill, this will let people know what allergies you have.

Allergies

Sometimes the body decides that a certain food isn't a good thing. It may be perfectly harmless, even healthy, for most people – like eggs, nuts, milk, or fish. But even the smallest nibble of the food can make a few allergic people very ill.

WHAT CAUSES ALLERGIES?

If disease-causing bacteria get into the body, the immune system releases special cells to try to fight off the intruders. But in some people, the immune system gets confused and attacks a particular food such as a peanut as if it were a dangerous "bug". In some cases these allergic reactions can be deadly.

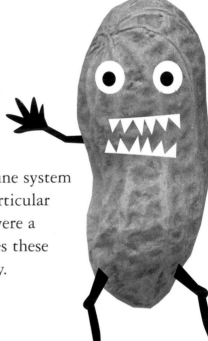

WHAT CAUSES INTOLERANCES?

Another type of reaction to eating the "wrong" things is called a food intolerance. This is different from an allergy, because it is not caused by the immune system, but by a fault in the way your body deals with food. However, although a food intolerance is an unpleasant nuisance, it is not dangerous.

A good example is dairy foods. If you have an intolerance to milk, drinking milk may cause symptoms like bloating and diarrhoea.

ALLERGIC REACTIONS

When the immune system reacts to a food it doesn't like, cells known as "mast cells" release a chemical called histamine into the blood. Histamine can cause an allergic reaction, which is when all kinds of uncomfortable symptoms may appear very suddenly.

These include *itchy eyes,* ***a runny nose,*** *skin rashes,* and *a swollen tongue.*

There is a very dangerous type of allergic reaction known as anaphylactic shock, which can happen at lightning speed. A person may be unable to breathe properly, and need emergency life-saving treatment. Anaphylactic shock isn't only triggered by eating something. In really serious cases, someone need only be near food they're allergic to, such as a bowl of nuts or shellfish, to become very seriously ill.

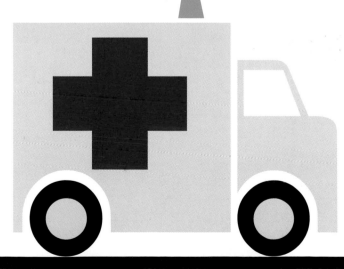

FOODS THAT MAY CAUSE PROBLEMS

While people can develop allergies or intolerances for many different foods (as well as many things that aren't food), the most common foods are:

Eggs, milk, peanuts, tree nuts, fish, shellfish, soy, and wheat.

Global differences

Certain allergies and intolerances can be more common in one part of the world than another. For example, milk contains a type of sugar that can be hard to digest. As babies, our bodies produce an enzyme called lactase, which makes digesting milk easier. But as we grow older we tend to produce less lactase, making milk harder to digest. People in Europe tend to continue producing lactase more than people in Asia and Africa do, so are less likely to develop a dairy intolerance.

HOW MUCH is enough?

Food is essential to every human, **without it** we simply **couldn't survive.** But it's important to stop and ask:

how much is enough?

FOOD gives you all the *energy* and *nutrients* you need to *grow and stay healthy*, but **too much food**, particularly the wrong food, can be a **bad thing**.

So watch what you eat, **choose wisely,** and *live well*.

For a smooth-running body, eat the right food.

BUSY BODY

You might think you only use energy when you move around, but most of your body's energy is actually used by your organs carrying out their basic functions. The brain alone uses roughly 19 per cent of your energy – mostly to send signals between brain cells; the rest is used to keep the cells healthy.

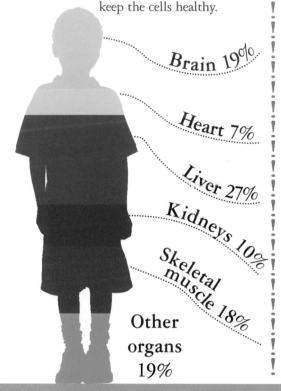

Brain 19%

Heart 7%

Liver 27%

Kidneys 10%

Skeletal muscle 18%

Other organs 19%

Using it up

The food we eat provides our body with energy to do things – running, walking, and even sleeping and thinking. But how much energy is needed to do all the things we do every day?

RELEASING YOUR ENERGY

The body uses all sorts of chemical processes to split up the molecules from food. As the molecules are broken down in the digestive system, or metabolized, they produce energy. Even when you're resting, your body is using energy. Around 70 per cent of your daily energy use is spent keeping your body systems running smoothly. Another 20 per cent is burned up by physical activity, and the remaining 10 per cent is used to metabolize food.

Storing energy
Excess energy from food that isn't used is stored in your body as fat. This can be useful as it's helpful to have a supply of energy. But too much can lead to health problems.

When awake, our brains produce *enough*

SLEEPING:
10 calories per 30 mins

Burning up energy

Your body uses most of your energy just to keep your body working, but different activities will use up even more. The amount of calories burned varies based on weight and age, but here are some rough numbers based on someone weighing 30kg (70lb).

SITTING:
17 calories per 30 mins

WALKING:
70 calories per 30 mins

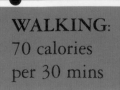

WHAT ARE CALORIES?

A calorie is simply a unit of energy. Specifically, the amount of energy needed to heat one gram of water by one degree Celsius. The number of calories on a food label shows how much potential energy the food has. The more calories a serving of food contains (usually listed as kJ or kcal) the more energy you will get from eating it. Because people are different sizes and burn energy at a different rate, there is no exact number for how many calories you should have, but most kids should aim for around 1,600–2,200 a day.

Slightly more than 350 calories (which is 6 apples) will fuel a brain for a day.

Calories in food

Different foods provide your body with a lot more energy than others. All of the following foods contain roughly 100 calories.

| 9 broccoli florets | 1 small baked potato | 1 medium egg | 20 cherries |

FAQ

What is a metabolic rate?

This is the rate at which your body "burns" your supply of energy, in the form of calories, when you're at rest.

What happens if a person eats too many calories?

If you eat more calories than you burn, the leftover energy is stored in your body as fat. If too much is stored you may gain weight and become unhealthy.

Are calories bad for you?

No, they are not. Your body needs calories to function. However, it's important to get your calories from foods that contain healthy nutrients.

What are empty calories?

This is a term given to foods that take a lot of energy to burn off but don't provide any extra nutrients. These are usually junk foods such as fizzy drinks, cakes, cookies, and crisps.

energy to power a small light bulb!

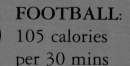

CYCLING:
120 calories
per 30 mins

FOOTBALL:
105 calories
per 30 mins

JOGGING:
120 calories
per 30 mins

SPRINTING:
245 calories
per 30 mins

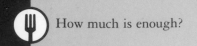

What's on your plate?

Food experts from around the world have created recommendations for the different types of food that you should include on your plate each day. The advice varies from country to country, but the experts all have the same aim – to encourage people to have healthy eating habits.

How much?

Although there are variations, the general advice is that carbohydrates, half of which should be wholegrains, make up a large part of the plate. Another wedge of the plate is vegetables and fruits, with more veg than fruit. Lean meat, fish, nuts, eggs, and low-fat dairy foods, are the smaller slices. Fats and sugars is the smallest slice, and these foods should be limited.

Fruits and Vegetables

This section should include more vegetables than fruit, and a variety of both. You get vitamins and minerals from these, and they protect you from health problems such as heart disease and cancer. Fruits and vegetables also protect you from infection, help you to heal, and maintain healthy skin.

Carbohydrates

Carbs are needed for growth, and to help our organs and muscles to work well. Carbs also provide our bodies with energy for work and play. Food with carbs includes pasta, bread, rice, cereal, and potatoes. When possible, choose wholegrain carbs such as wholemeal bread and brown rice.

Eat vegetables in abundance

Fruits and Vegetables

Carbohydrates

UK "Eatwell Plate"

The proportions should be equal for fruits and vegetables and carbohydrates. Then protein and dairy take the next big chunks on the plate. The smallest section is reserved for fats and sugars, which should be kept to a minimum.

US "My Plate"

Make half of your plate fruits and vegetables (with more vegetables than fruit). One-quarter of your plate should be grains (try to choose wholegrains) and one-quarter should be protein. In addition, it suggests a portion of dairy foods. Skimmed milk and low fat cheese are best.

"Food Pyramids"

A popular graphic way to show proportions is the "Food Pyramid". The bottom layer represents breads and grains, the next layer is veg and fruits, followed by protein, then dairy, and lastly a small section for fats, oils, and sweets. The latter should be eaten sparingly.

Enjoy fruit of every colour

Dairy

Fats and Sugars

Protein

Dairy

Dairy includes milk, cheese, and yogurt. Dairy products are high in calcium. This is a mineral that helps to build and strengthen bones and teeth. It also helps the nerves and muscles to work properly.

Fats and Sugars

Fats produce energy, and are fine in small amounts, but too much fat can be bad, leading to weight gain and health problems. Foods with unhealthy fats include chocolate, ice cream, cheese, whole milk, butter, fatty meat, and cookies. Healthy fats such as avocado, olive, and nut oils should be a part of your daily diet. Refined sugar isn't really needed in the diet, but it makes foods taste nice.

Protein

Protein helps to build and repair cells and muscles. Examples of protein-rich foods include lean meat, lentils, beans, chicken, fish, eggs, and soya products.

Eat fruit *and* veg

Fruits and vegetables taste delicious and add flavour and texture to your meals, but why is it a good idea to eat a lot of them? It's because they are considered to be an important part of a healthy diet.

FOUR REASONS TO EAT UP

1 Fruits and vegetables are a great source of minerals and vitamins, including vitamin C, folic acid, and potassium. All of these lead to good health.

2 Eating a healthy amount of fruits and vegetables each day can help to prevent and reduce the risk of stroke, heart disease, and some cancers.

3 They help to ensure you get enough dietary fibre, which prevents digestive problems such as constipation. A diet high in fibre can also reduce the risk of bowel cancer.

4 Vegetables and fruits are generally low in fat and calories, so they play a vital role in helping people to maintain a healthy weight.

WHICH ONES COUNT?

Almost all fresh fruits and vegetables count, as well as fruit canned in natural juice, canned veg, frozen fruit and veg, and also dried fruits.

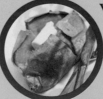

Do drinks count?

Yes, 150ml (⅓ pt) 100 per cent fruit or vegetable juice will count as one serving. However, they can't be your only source. Some smoothies may count as two servings.

What about potatoes?

Unfortunately, they don't count because they are full of starch. The same goes for yams and cassava. However, sweet potatoes, parsnips, and swedes all count.

Are frozen fruit or veg okay?

Yes, it doesn't have to always be fresh. Even ice lollies made from natural fruit juice or purée are a part of your allowance. The same goes for dried fruit.

An easy way to up your intake is to snack

GLOBAL SUGGESTIONS

Many countries, such as the UK, France, Sweden, Germany, and Austria recommend at least five portions of a variety of fruit and veg a day. The Swiss also suggest five, but say that a variety of colours is key.

Is five enough? Some experts suggest the number should actually be seven. Other countries such as Canada, don't give a number, and instead say that fruit and veg should make up half of your plate.

Different countries have varying guidelines on the minimum fruit and veg we should eat each day, *BUT* they all agree on one thing...

...we need to eat more fruit and veg!

In Australia, the advice is to eat more vegetables because fruit contains more sugar. They suggest two fruit and five veg. In Greece, it's three portions of fruit and six portions of veg.

Scientific studies have been carried out to see if an even greater number, would have an impact on benefits to your health, but the results have been inconclusive. So in the US they simply say "more matters", and variety is important.

Can I have a can of fruit? Yes, if added sugar or salt aren't in the list of ingredients. Fruit canned in its own juice, rather than syrup, is fine. As are veg canned in water (with no added sugar, salt, or fat).

Does it have to be cooked? Cooked fruit and veg count toward your allowance, but snacking on raw vegetables such as carrots is good as well, and counts towards your goal.

Beans and pulses? As with drinks, a maximum of one portion of beans and pulses are recommended. Try adding beans and pulses to soups and salads.

on *fruit and veg* THROUGHOUT the day.

maximum 5–8 teaspoons recommended per day

The average western teenager

How can I spot added sugar on the label?

Look for names ending in "ose", such as sucrose, fructose, glucose, dextrose, and lactose. But also look out for cane juice, honey, maple syrup, and molasses.

Are any sugars sweeter than others?

Fructose is sweeter than other simple sugars, so you need less, and that means fewer calories.

Why is sugar added?

To make it appeal to the consumer – you! Manufacturers like sugar because it's a cheap additive. It accentuates flavour, helps to preserve the food, and improves its shelf-life. Also, they know you often like to have a sweet treat!

You love the sweet stuff, and you may eat more than you should, knowing it isn't good for you. Now it's official: too much sugar isn't just making kids fat – it's making them sick.

Too SWEET?

The World Health Organization has warned of eating too much sugar. They are hugely concerned that excess sugar is causing obesity, leading to diseases such as diabetes and heart disease. It's affecting half a billion people in the world, particularly kids. The situation is so bad that doctors are predicting that this generation may not live as long as their parents.

One average can of cola = 9 teaspoons of sugar

9 boiled sweets = 8 teaspoons sugar

consumes 32 teaspoons of sugar a day

WHICH FOODS HAVE ADDED SUGAR?

Just about all processed foods contain added sugar – it's the number one additive. Although you expect it to be in sweet foods, it pops up in some unlikely places.

Sugar is often added to savoury foods such as pizza, soup, hot dogs, and ketchup. It even appears in crackers, spaghetti sauce, lunch meat, canned vegetables, salad dressing, mayonnaise, and some peanut butters.

So why add it to savoury foods? Because a little sugar can reduce salty or sour flavours. Too much just makes the food taste sweet, so the manufacturers have to be careful how much they add.

What does sugar do?

Too much can cause tooth decay, and weight gain, which increases the risk of diabetes. It may boost your mood, which could explain why people crave sugar.

Why do I like it?

• Eating sugar gives an instant lift. However, the feeling of satisfaction and pleasure may be followed by an energy crash.
• The love for sugar may be an evolutionary hangover; kids who liked high-energy foods would have had a better chance of survival.

What are "empty calories"? That means me – I don't have any other nutrients! But if you want a treat now and then, I taste good!

I've got a better flavour and I'm less processed. But like my pal – I don't have any other nutrients!

One 60g (2oz) bar milk chocolate = 7 teaspoons of sugar

WHAT DOES FAT DO TO ME?

Fat in food can lead to weight gain faster than anything else. That's because fat has more energy per gram than any other food group. And the wrong fats, such as trans fats or too much saturated fat, can be harmful to health.

FAQ

So how much fat should kids have in a day?

Guidelines suggest that boys of 11–14 need 2,220 calories each day; girls of the same age need 1,845 calories every day. Fat should provide no more than 30–35 per cent of daily energy (calories). Saturated fat, the fat found in animal products, should provide no more than 11 per cent of daily energy (calories).

Why should I eat burgers and fries only sometimes?

Because of the fat content. The average cheeseburger has around 6g of saturated fat, and fries have 2g. For just a fast lunch, you will have consumed 40 percent of your recommended daily intake of saturated fats.

Too fatty?

It seems that fat is in all your favourite foods. Ice cream, burgers, pizza, and doughnuts all contain a lot of fat. A typical meaty pizza may contain 2 tsp of fat in each slice – about one-third of the safe saturated fat allowance. But will you stop at one slice? If you are tempted to have two more, you'll have eaten your entire fat allowance for the day.

WHY IS FAT ADDED?

Fat makes food taste good, and it feels nice in your mouth. Food producers know this, and they know you will want more once you have tasted the food. Processed food hasn't got much flavour, so manufacturers add some fat to give a crisp or moist finish to baked foods – and a tasty flavour. And of course, deep-fried foods are coated in a lot of fat.

4 million fat cells store the *energy* of 0.1g fat.

maximum 6 teaspoons unsaturated oil recommended per day

maximum 6 grams (1tsp) salt per day
for adults, less for children

Too salty?

You need only a very small amount of salt in your diet.
Because around 80 per cent of your salt intake may be from
hidden salt, or salt you haven't added, it's easy to have too
much. It's always a good idea to check the label for salt or
sodium content before buying. If you start with fresh foods,
you can control how much salt is added.

WHY IS SALT ADDED?

Salt seems to make everything taste better. It can suppress
bitter tastes, and, surprisingly, can even enhance the flavour
and make sweet foods seem sweeter! Our taste buds seem
tuned to like salt, so it's not surprising that food companies
add salt to everything; it makes bland food taste better, and
adds flavour to most foods. Maybe that's why even sweet
foods have some salt added. Another reason is that salt is
cheap, which keeps costs down. It adds flavour, and helps
to preserve the product and improve its shelf life.

WHAT DOES SALT DO TO ME?

Too much salt can cause a water salt imbalance in the body,
and high blood pressure problems. Continuing to have too
much can cause long-term damage such as heart disease.

FAQ

Is sodium the same as salt?

Salt is 40% sodium and 60% chloride.
On food labels, you may find sodium
listed, but you can easily convert
sodium to salt. 400mg of sodium is
equivalent to 1g salt, which is a good
pinch of salt.

**How much sodium or salt
do we need each day to stay
healthy?**

Only tiny amounts are needed. Sodium
intake should be no more than 1,600mg
sodium per day, or 4g salt. Salt has
already been added to a lot of everyday
foods such as bacon, cheese, ready
meals, sauces, and soups. After birth we
prefer sweet foods. A liking for salt has
to be learned, so that means we can get
used to the taste of food without salt.

A small bag of crisps
contains one-tenth
of your daily salt
requirements.

Taste *before* adding salt, you may not need it!

Look at the label

Daily values

This is a guide to nutrients in one serving. (It's also called reference intake (RI).) For example, 2% dietary fibre means that one serving provides 2% of the fibre needed daily. Per cent daily values are based on a 2,000-calorie diet for a healthy adult.

Serving size

Serving size and the number of servings are suggested on the label, but they may be different from what you think of as a serving size. The size will tell you how many calories and nutrients there are in one serving.

Energy

The amount of calories per serving and calories from fat is shown here. Some labels show the amount of energy and the amount per portion as kj and kcal.

Other nutrients

Generally the following are listed: total fat, saturated fat, sodium, carbohydrates, dietary fibre, sugars, protein, vitamin A, vitamin C, iron, and calcium. Some labels also include cholesterol, and trans fats.

Sodium

The daily intake of sodium is recommended to be no more than 6g, so the amount of sodium in a biscuit is fairly low. Sodium is simply part of salt.

CHOCOLATE CHIP COOKIES

NUTRITIONAL INFORMATION

Serving size 28g (1oz)

Amount per serving 1 cookie

Calories 120	Calories from fat 45

		% Daily value*
Total Fat	5g	8%
Saturated Fat	2.5g	12%
Trans Fat	0g	
Cholesterol	10g	3%
Sodium	120mg	5%
Total Carbohydrate	18g	6%
Dietary Fibre	1g	2%
Sugars	11g	
Protein	1g	

Vitamin A	0%
Vitamin C	0%
Calcium	0%
Iron	4%

*The percent daily value may be higher or lower depending on your needs. The amounts of nutrients are maximum, "less than" is recommended for all. The amounts of total carbohydrate and dietary fibre are minimum amounts.

Recommended daily intakes		2,000 calories	2,500 calories
Total Fat	Less than	65g	80g
Saturated Fat	Less than	20g	25g
Cholesterol	Less than	300mg	300mg
Sodium	Less than	2,400mg	2,400mg
Total Carbohydrate		300g	375g
Dietary Fibre		25g	30g

Avoid food that lists different *sugars first* – it *probably*

When you want to know what's in your food, look at the label! Most pre-packed foods list ingredients in order of weight, so the main ingredient comes first. By looking at the label you can compare foods and choose the one that is healthier by avoiding those that list sugar or fat as the first ingredient.

INGREDIENTS

- Flour (bleached white flour, malted barley flour)
- Niacin
- Reduced iron
- Potassium bromate
- Thiamine mononitrate
- Riboflavin
- Folic acid
- Brown sugar
- Chocolate drops
- Sugar • Eggs
- Soy grade margarine (soy lecithin, interesterified soy bean oil) • Vitamin A palmitate • Palm oil
- Vanilla extract • Salt
- Bicarbonate of soda

Names for sugar

Sugar can have many names on labels. These include maltose, dextrose, sucrose, honey, maple syrup, corn syrup, molasses, high fructose corn syrup, and fruit juice concentrate.

Soy lecithin

This is an emulsifier that makes oil and water mix together. In chocolate cookies, it stops the fatty cocoa butter from separating.

Interesterified soy bean oil

Since trans fats have been exposed as dangerous to health, this oil is used as a replacement. The oil is chemically altered and, like trans fats, its use raises health concerns.

Artificial flavourings

In a food such as chocolate biscuits, vanilla extract is added. It has a strong odour and is much cheaper than real vanilla. Propylene glycol, a compound used in anti-freeze, is sometimes added to prolong shelf-life.

Colour coding

In some countries, nutrition labels use a traffic lights system. The ingredients are colour coded red, amber, or green. Healthier foods have more greens and ambers, and fewer reds.

Red on a label means that the product is high in fat, saturated fat, salt, or sugars. Try to eat these less often and only in small amounts.

Amber means medium – it's neither high nor low. Go for more ambers than reds.

Green means low fat, saturated fat, sugars, and salt. More green is better.

WHY NOT MAKE YOUR OWN?

Homemade choc chip cookies:

You will need just 6 ingredients!

- 225g (8oz) self- raising flour • 200g (7oz) chocolate
- 125g (4½oz) polyunsaturated spread • 100g (3½oz) brown sugar
- 1 egg • 1½ tsp vanilla extract

won't be a good choice.

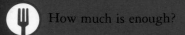

BIGGER

THEN

The size of the average dinner plate was 21.5cm (8½in) in diameter. This size of plate held about 800 calories of food. It meant that in one sitting, people ate less than they do today.

NOW

The size of the average dinner plate is now 30cm (12in) in diameter. It can hold about 1,900 calories. One reason why people are larger and heavier than ever is that portions are much bigger.

1960s

2015

> Eating too much is bad for digestion. Your liver can only process nutrients at a certain rate.

> The average fast-food burger contains almost double the calories it had less than 50 years ago.

PLATE INFLATION

The size of the average dinner plate has increased greatly in the past fifty years, and once people get used to eating larger portions, it's hard to go back.

is not BETTER

Studies show that people eat more food when presented with bigger portions. The increase in portion size and amount we eat in recent years is one of the reasons why people weigh more than previous generations.

A HANDY GUIDE

Everybody is different, so estimating the right portion sizes can be tricky. An easy way to work things out is to follow the "Hand Diet". The plan suggests portion sizes equivalent to different parts of your hand. The bigger a person's hand is, the bigger the portion they're allowed.

FIST

The size of a clenched fist is a good guide for portions of carbohydrates, raw vegetables, fresh fruit, or salad.

FINGERTIP

The size of your fingertip is a good rough suggestion for the amount of butter, margarine, mayonnaise, and oils to have in any one sitting. For example, it's the right amount of butter to spread on your toast.

I WISH I HAD BIGGER HANDS!

THUMB

The size of your thumb (down to your knuckle) is an indicator of the maximum portion you should have of foods such as cream cheese, salad dressing, sour cream, peanut butter, and hard cheeses.

PALM

The size of your palm indicates the suggested amount of meat, poultry, and fish to have as a single portion.

It can take *20 minutes* before your *brain receives the signal* from your stomach that it's full, *so try to eat slowly* so you don't have too much.

TYPES OF ADDITIVES

Preservatives

Food preservatives are added to prevent the growth of bacteria and moulds, to stop fats and oils getting rancid, and to help retain colour, flavour, and texture.

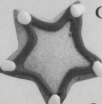

Colours

Adding colour makes food look more appealing to eat, especially if the natural colour has been lost during processing.

Sweeteners

Added sweeteners can be natural or artificial. Often found in slimming products, artificial sweeteners are hundreds of times sweeter than natural sugars, so have to be used in small amounts. Natural sugars add bulk to foods such as cakes and biscuits.

Nutrients

Vitamins and minerals may be added to replace those lost through processing. Iodine, which is needed for healthy thyroid function, is sometimes added to salt for those whose soil lacks iodine.

Emulsifiers

These are added to foods to stop mixtures turning back into separate liquids. Salad dressings, ice-cream, peanut butter, and mayonnaise all contain emulsifiers.

Stabilizers and thickeners

These additives create a firm, even texture and smooth taste in foods such as sauces, jams, dairy, cakes, and puddings. They also stop them separating and increase the storage qualities.

Flavourings

Both natural or artificial flavourings are used to replace flavours lost in processing, or to make dull food tasty. "Enhancers" such as monosodium glutamate are used to bring out natural flavours.

Added *extras*

Cooking with fresh, natural ingredients is the ideal way to eat. But it can be hard to find time to choose ingredients and prepare meals. It's easier to grab a ready-made burger, but *what really goes into it?*

Most foods go through some processing, and can lose texture, colour, flavour, and nutrients along the way. To make food look and taste good, and to keep it fresher for longer, extra ingredients are often added. These additives can be natural or artificial, and while they are approved for food use, some additions seem rather strange. For example, titanium dioxide, used to add colour to food, is also found in paints and sunscreen!

WHAT'S IN YOUR COLA?

INGREDIENTS

Carbonated water, sugar, colour, phosphoric acid (a preservative that adds a sharp flavour), natural flavourings, including caffeine.

ADDED EXTRAS

This varies from country to country, but include sugar, glycerine, neroli oil (orange aroma), citric acid, and sodium citrate (for tart flavour).

Hold the additives!

WHAT ELSE IS IN A FAST-FOOD BURGER?

BURGER BUN
INGREDIENTS: flour (nutrient enriched), water, yeast, salt, sugar, sunflower oil, sesame seeds, rapeseed oil
ADDITIVES: vitamin C (lightens dough), silicon dioxide (anti-caking agent), calcium peroxide (bleaching agent), sorbitol (sweetener), dextrin (for flavour and crispness)

PICKLES
INGREDIENTS: cucumbers, water, distilled vinegar, salt
ADDITIVES: calcium chloride (firming agent), potassium aluminium sulphate (stabilizer)

ONIONS
INGREDIENTS: chopped onions, vegetable oil

CHEESE
INGREDIENTS: milk, salt, water, annatto colouring
ADDITIVES: soy protein, sodium citrate (binder), sodium phosphate (foaming agent), potassium sorbate (preservative), citric acid (acidity), lipase (flavour enhancer)

BEEF BURGER
INGREDIENTS: ground beef, salt, pepper
ADDITIVES: rusk, water, stabilizers, beef fat, egg, seasoning, salt

LETTUCE
INGREDIENTS: leaf lettuce

KETCHUP
INGREDIENTS: tomatoes, sugar, white vinegar, salt, spices, onion powder
ADDITIVES: sugar

MUSTARD SAUCE
INGREDIENTS: mustard seed, vinegar, sugar, salt, spices, water
ADDITIVES: food starch, xanthan gum (thickener), propylene glycol alginate (stabilizers), titanium dioxide (colour), sodium benzoate (prevents moulds)

Fast-food secrets revealed

Making it *last*

When you hear the words "processed foods", you may not think of it as a good thing. However, most foods you eat have been processed in some way. Food is perishable, and will eventually rot, so processing plays a vital role in making food last longer and keeping it safe to eat. While most food processing is carried out to extend its shelf life and make it safe, too much processing can have a definite downside.

PROS

- Processing prevents *spoilage*.

- It *destroys* germs and dangerous chemicals.

- *Seasonal produce* can be eaten later in the year.

- Some foods are *inedible* in their raw form.

- Extra *nutrients* can be added.

- Food becomes available to a *wider range* of people.

CONS

- Processing food can cause it to *lose natural nutrients* and vitamins.

- *Preservatives* are often high in sugar, salt, fat, or artificial additives.

- There is a risk of contamination *at every stage* of the process.

- It may encourage *unhealthy eating* habits.

- People lose the skill of cooking.

PREHISTORIC PRESERVING

Food has always been precious. Throughout history, people gathered food when it was plentiful and found ways to keep it for many long months until it became available again. Even as far back as prehistoric times, there have been crude forms of food processing. The discovery of fire gave us cooking and smoking.

PRESERVING METHODS

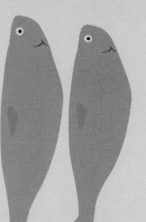

Smoking
Although smoking was first used as a way to preserve food, now it is something of a delicacy. Most meat and any fish can be smoked, but oily fish such as salmon or trout absorb more of the wood-smoke flavour.

Drying
The method of drying food to preserve it has been used for thousands of years. Vegetables and fruit are left outside to dry naturally in the sun and wind.

Sun-dried tomatoes

Sugar
Food is stored in sugar to help preserve it. The sugar is used in a syrupy form to help preserve fruit, such as pears, apples, and peaches.

Pickling
Foods can be pickled in vinegar — an acid that bacteria don't like — or a salt solution. This encourages the growth of good bacteria during fermentation. Pickling can also add a tasty sour flavour to food.

Canning
Cans are heated to sterilize the contents. Food to be canned is cooked then sealed in the sterile cans. This process is called sterilization.

Meat, fruit, milk, and vegetables can be preserved by canning.

Bottling
Foods that are highly acidic, such as fruits and vegetables, can be bottled, because bacteria are less likely to grow in acidic conditions. However, there is a danger that mould can grow.

Dehydration
This is a way of keeping food fresh by removing moisture. Products that are often dehydrated include powdered milk, dried fruits, vegetables, pasta, and instant rice.

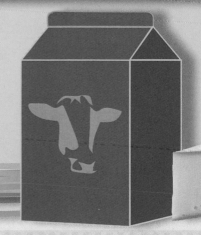

Pasteurizing
This is a technique that preserves liquid foods. For example, milk is heated to 70°C (158°F) for a short time in order to kill off bacteria.

Freezing

When food is frozen it can be kept up to six months: some foods can be kept for longer. Advice is usually given on the packaging.

Vacuum packs
Food can be sealed in bags with all the air sucked out of them so that microorganisms can't get in. Vacuum packing is often used for nuts and fruit.

FUTURE *food*

A rising population

The global population has risen a lot over the last few centuries, from only around 1 billion people in 1800 to around 7 billion today. It's also growing faster than ever.

1800
1 billion
people

1950
2.5 billion
people

Back in the middle of the 20th century, it was imagined that by 2050 we wouldn't need to cook and prepare food – we would simply pop a pill that would supply us with all the nutrients we need. That is still a long way off, but the question remains: *how will we feed ourselves in the future?*

POPPING A PILL

Scientists have attempted to produce a pill to include all the essential nutrients. Unfortunately it proved hard to cram around 2,000 calories into one capsule. Each would have weighed around 225 g (½ lb) and would have been almost impossible to swallow.

Dinner MONDAY

Breakfast TUESDAY

Dinner TUESDAY

Breakfast MONDAY

Lunch SUNDAY

Lunch TUESDAY

Lunch MONDAY

Between 30–50% of food produced globally is wasted

INSECTS

Some insects actually contain more nutrients than meat. The problem is changing peoples' perception of eating creepy crawlies for dinner. Already 2 billion people regularly eat insects; the other 5 billion aren't so keen. Around 1,400 species are edible, including grasshoppers, witchetty grubs, weevils, termites, and mealworms. They are high in protein, vitamins, and minerals, and can be grown in small spaces.

I'm nutritious and taste better than you might think

Breakfast THURSDAY

Dinner SUNDAY

Lunch FRIDAY

Lunch THURSDAY

It takes 8kg (17lb) of feed to make 1kg (2lb) of beef, but 1.7kg (4lb) feed to make 1kg (2lb) of cricket meat.

What will be on your

They could be ground up and made into burgers or sausages.

One of the *greatest challenges* of the future will be simply growing enough to *feed an increasing population.*

2015 7 billion people

♟♟♟♟♟♟♟

2050 9 billion people

♟♟♟♟♟♟♟♟♟

RISING DEMAND

The population is expected to rise from 7 billion in 2015, to more than 9 billion by 2050. This will be a big problem because it is estimated that we will need almost twice as much food to feed the planet. There is only a limited amount of land that is suitable for farming, and we're already using most of it. Increased farming would mean more deforestation, and using 70 per cent of available freshwater.

ALGAE

Certain algae are highly nutritious, containing protein, vitamins, and antioxidants. Algae are fast-growing organisms ranging in size from tiny single cells to 61-m (200-ft) long giant kelp seaweeds. They don't need land but can grow in seawater, as well as in some polluted water. Seaweeds are eaten in some countries, but other types could be used as processed foods for humans, as feed for animals, or even as fertilizer.

Artificial steak made in a laboratory may be a way to go

LAB FOOD

Making food artificially in the laboratory is a plan scientists have come up with to solve food shortage. Imagine a printer in your kitchen that produces a juicy steak at the touch of a button. This idea is closer than you think. 3D printers that make things out of plastic already exist. By adapting this technology to take stem cells (specialized body cells that can be turned into muscle, skin, or other organ tissue) instead of plastic, cells can be squirted out and printed into a shape. The cells then fuse together to form edible tissue.

plate in 2050?

Food QUIZ

How much do you really know about food and nutrition? Find out by taking this quiz. Questions relate to ingredients, digestion, and nutrition.

1 Where does the digestive process start?
- A) Stomach
- B) Oesophagus
- C) Mouth

2 What fruit did sailors eat to prevent scurvy?
- A) Oranges
- B) Apples
- C) Limes

3 Which country does paella come from?
- A) France
- B) Spain
- C) Egypt

4 What's another name for maize?
- A) Flour
- B) Corn
- C) Spelt

5 What is the main nutrient in pasta and bread?
- A) Carbohydrates
- B) Proteins
- C) Sugars

6 Which fruit do you use to make Halloween lanterns?
- A) Sweet potato
- B) Butternut squash
- C) Pumpkin

7 Where do potatoes grow?
- A) On trees
- B) Underground
- C) On a vine

8 What is the main ingredient of cheese?
- A) Yogurt
- B) Milk
- C) Custard

9 How often should you eat oily fish?
- A) Twice a week
- B) Each day
- C) Once a week

10 Which fat is least healthy?
- A) Monounsaturated
- B) Polyunsaturated
- C) Saturated

11 Do you know how many cells are in your body?
- A) Billions
- B) Millions
- C) Trillions

12 What is celeriac?
- A) A fruit
- B) A vegetable
- C) A celery-like vegetable

13 Which sweet food is made by bees?
- A) Syrup
- B) Candy
- C) Honey

14 Which fruit won't continue ripening once picked?
- A) Raspberries
- B) Plums
- C) Blueberries

15 Is salt bad for you?
- A) Yes
- B) No
- C) It depends how much

16 What are trans fats used in?
- A) Smoothies and fruit juices
- B) Crisps and cakes
- C) Salads and soups

17 What does "Fe" stand for?
- A) Iron
- B) Copper
- C) Zinc

18 What is a dangerous allergic reaction called?
- A) Anaphylactic
- B) Acrobatic
- C) Magnetic

I know some of these! Answers are on page 94.

Hmmm, tricky!

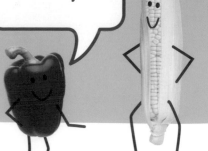

88

Picture QUIZ

QUIZ

1 What is this?
A) Bugs eating jam
B) A strawberry
C) Sesame seeds in sauce

2 What are these?
A) Insects hatching out
B) Cashew nuts
C) Exotic fruit

3 Do you know what this is?
A) Mackerel
B) Snake skin
C) Fisherman's net

4 What do you think this strange creature is?
A) Alien from outer space
B) Dragon fruit
C) Radish

5 What are these?
A) Mini aubergines
B) Giant grapes
C) Purple potatoes

6 What is this?
A) Forest of Christmas trees
B) Alien plant
C) Cauliflower

> ### Are these TRUE or FALSE?

1 Chickens can fly.

2 The average chicken lays 260 eggs in a year.

3 The world's heaviest turkey weighed 75kg (165lb).

4 Eight medium omelettes can be made from one ostrich egg.

5 There are 1 billion domestic chickens in the world.

6 We obtain iron from dark leafy greens, red meat, liver, and shellfish.

7 Baking powder is often added to cakes to make them rise.

8 Popcorn kernels can pop as high as a three-storey building.

9 Frying is the best way of preserving nutrients in vegetables.

10 Potatoes were first cultivated in Peru.

> What could that be?

Glossary

Additive A natural or artificial chemical added to food to make it keep longer, look and taste nicer, or provide better nutrition.

Amino acid One of the tiny building blocks that make up proteins.

Amylase An enzyme in the saliva that helps digest starch.

Antioxidant A nutrient, found in fruits, vegetables, wholegrains, and legumes that helps to stop harmful substances called free radicals causing damage to the body.

Artificial flavourings Natural or synthetic chemicals that are added to foods to give a specific taste.

Bile A fluid that helps us digest fats. Made in the liver and stored in the gall bladder, bile flows into the small intestine when food is eaten as part of the digestive process.

Borborygmi The word used to describe the sound of a stomach rumbling.

Calcium A mineral that is important for building healthy bones and teeth.

Calorie A unit of energy contained in food.

Carbohydrates Types of nutrients that turn into glucose (sugar) when eaten. They are the body's most important source of fuel and energy.

Cell membrane A thin skin that holds cells together. It also controls what goes in and out of a cell.

Cellulose The substance that builds the cell walls of plants and gives them support. Processed cellulose is used as a food additive to improve both texture and bulk.

Cholesterol A fat-like substance found in blood and body cells. Some cholesterol is made in the liver and some comes from food.

Chyme The slushy mixture of partly digested food that is squeezed from the stomach into the top part of the small intestine.

Cytoplasm A jelly-like substance outside the nucleus, in every living cell of the body.

Diabetes A disease in which there is too much sugar in the blood. A hormone called insulin, which is made in the pancreas, opens up the cells of the body so that sugar from the blood can get in. Over time, if there's not enough insulin, the sugar in the blood rises and causes diabetes.

Digestive enzymes Chemicals produced in various parts of the digestive system to help break down food.

Digestive system The long passageway from mouth to anus, together with the liver, gall bladder, and pancreas.

DNA The abbreviation for deoxyribonucleic acid, a molecule found in every cell in the body. Like a computer program, DNA is loaded with coded instructions which tell each of our cells what to do.

Emulsifier An additive used to stop liquids – such as oil and water – separating from one another in a mixture.

Energy You need energy for work, rest, and play. It is also used by the body for growth and repair.

Enhancer A substance such as salt or monosodium glutamate (MSG) that is added to food to improve its flavour.

Enzyme A biological agent in the body that speeds up reactions. Enzymes play a part in digestion, breaking up big molecules in food into small ones that can be absorbed for energy.

Fats These act as a store of energy that your body can use if it runs out of carbohydrates.

Fatty acids These are produced when fatty foods, such as meat or cheese, are broken down in the digestive system. When fatty acids are absorbed into the bloodstream they provide energy.

Fermentation A chemical change caused by tiny bacteria, yeast, or mould breaking down foods. Fermentation can cause several reactions including making bread rise, or milk sour.

Fibre The part of plant foods (including fruits, vegetables, and grains) that pass through the digestive system without being broken down.

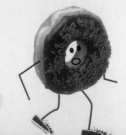

Folic acid One of the B vitamins, folic acid is vital for making red and white blood cells, and helps the body use protein. It is also used to make DNA in the body's cells.

Food allergy An unusual reaction by the body's immune system to a particular food. Symptoms may include itchy skin rashes, stomach upsets, and a wheezy chest. In a very dangerous reaction known as anaphylaxis, a person may be unable to breathe.

Food intolerance The inability of the digestive system to break down certain types of food properly. Intolerance may cause sickness, diarrhoea, stomach pain, and bloating.

Food processing The methods by which raw food is made suitable for humans to eat, cook, or store.

Free radicals Unstable molecules in the body that may damage normal cells and lead to health problems.

Fructose A simple sugar found in fruit and vegetables. It is known as the fruit sugar. Part of the sugar in honey is fructose.

Gall bladder A small, bag-like organ just under the liver. It holds bile, a digestive fluid made in the liver.

Ghrelin A hormone that controls your appetite. It is mainly produced by the stomach. Its levels increase rapidly when you need to eat, then decrease after a meal. Ghrelin also stimulates growth hormones.

Glucose A type of sugar, obtained from many foods, that is used by the body for energy.

Glycogen Extra glucose (sugar) that is stored in the liver and muscles ready to be used quickly when our energy levels start to drop.

Histamine A chemical occurring naturally in body cells that is involved in allergic reactions. When released from the cells, it can cause sneezing and runny eyes.

Hormones Various chemicals made in the body that help all our internal systems to work properly.

Hypothalamus The part of the brain that is responsible for hormone production.

Immune system The body's defence system, which uses special blood cells and fluids to help fight off germs and protect us against illness.

Insulin A hormone made in the pancreas that regulates blood sugar.

Junk food Foods that provide very little nourishment but often contain unhealthy amounts of sugar, salt, and other additives. These can include crisps, biscuits, and fizzy drinks.

Lean If describing meat, it means it contains little or no fat.

Leptin A hormone produced by the intestines that tells the brain when your body has enough stored energy. This tells you when to stop eating.

Lipids Fatty, oily, or waxy substances that occur naturally in the body and hold large stores of energy.

Liver An organ on the right side of the body. It helps process food and filters harmful substances from the blood.

Lycopene A helpful chemical in tomatoes, guava, and sweet red peppers that acts as an antioxidant. It is released by cooking, so there is more lycopene in cooked tomatoes than in raw tomatoes.

Macrominerals A group of minerals that the body needs in large quantities. The group includes magnesium, calcium, potassium, phosphorus, and sulphur.

Metabolism All the chemical processes that go on within the body. This term is especially used to describe how the body deals with the food we put into it.

Mineral A nutrient such as calcium, iron, potassium, and sodium that are essential for health. The body can't make minerals, so gets them from food.

Mitochondria The powerhouses of the cells. They act like a digestive system, taking in nutrients, breaking them down, and creating energy for the cell.

Molecule A tiny substance formed from two or more atoms. Just about everything, including our bodies, is made up of molecules.

Nucleus This is the control centre of a cell; it sends instructions to the rest of the cell telling it what chemicals to make.

Nutrients Substances provided by food that the body needs for nourishment and growth.

Obesity This means that a person is too heavy for their height. Health problems such as diabetes and heart disease can result from obesity.

Oesophagus The long tube from the mouth to the stomach that food travels down when we swallow.

Organ A part of the body that has a particular job to do. The digestive organs are the stomach, intestines, liver, pancreas, and gallbladder.

Pancreas An organ in the upper part of the digestive system. It produces a hormone called insulin that regulates the level of glucose in the blood.

Pasteurization A method that preserves milk, beer, and wine by exposing them to high temperatures.

Peristalsis Wave-like movements in the lining of the intestines, created by regular tightening and relaxing of muscles. This pushes food along the digestive tract.

Phytonutrients Chemicals found in plant foods that give protection against free radicals – molecules that can stop body cells from working properly and cause illness.

Preservative Extra substances added to processed food to make it last longer. Preservatives can be natural, like salt or vinegar, or man-made.

Protein A nutrient made from chemicals called amino acids that are joined together in chains. Protein contains various elements, such as carbon, oxygen, and nitrogen. Protein is essential for growth and repair.

Roughage Another word for fibre. It keeps your digestive system healthy and working well.

Saliva A watery fluid produced in the mouth. It moistens food so that it can be swallowed easily. Saliva contains substances called enzymes, which begin the process of digestion.

Saturated fat So-called "bad" fat, found in meat and dairy products, and many processed foods. Eating too much of it is thought to raise levels of cholesterol in the blood and increase the risk of heart disease.

Sodium A mineral found in most foods. While the body needs sodium to work properly, too much can have a bad effect, causing high blood pressure and even heart disease and stroke.

Stabilizer A substance added to processed food to give it a smoother, firmer texture.

Starch A type of carbohydrate found in foods such as bread, pasta, potatoes, and cereals.

Sugar A type of carbohydrate that provides a quick source of energy. Natural sugars come from many foods, especially fruit. Refined sugars are a common food additive.

Teflon A coating on saucepans and baking trays that stops food from sticking.

Tissues Groups of similar cells that perform a common function.

Toxin A poisonous substance that can make you ill.

Trace minerals These are minerals that are needed in tiny amounts. They include iron, chromium, fluoride, zinc, manganese, and selenium.

Trans fat A type of fat made when oils are chemically changed into solid substances. This kind of fat is found in products such as margarine, biscuits, pies, cakes, and many processed snack foods. Trans fat increases cholesterol levels in the body, which is unhealthy for your heart.

Unsaturated fat Known as "good" fat, this lowers cholesterol levels and is important to health. It is found in oily fish such as salmon and sardines, and many plant foods, including nuts, olive oil, and avocados.

Villi Tiny finger-like projections that line the small intestine. They have a large surface area, and a good blood supply. Their function is to absorb food efficiently into the bloodstream.

Vitamins Various nutrients essential for good health. They keep many vital processes in the body working. Most vitamins come from plant and animal food and cannot be stored in the body, although there are some that the body can make as well.

Water About 60 per cent of your body is made of water. Every chemical reaction, such as digestion, needs water, so it is very important.

Index

All happiness depends on ... breakfast.

Answers

Page 47	Page 88	16. B	Page 89
1. A	FOOD QUIZ	17. A	TRUE or FALSE
2. A	1. C	18. A	1. True
3. C	2. C		2. True
4. C	3. B		3. False – it weighed 40kg (88lb).
5. B	4. B	Page 89	4. True
	5. A	PICTURE QUIZ	5. False – there are 25 billion.
Page 53	6. C	1. B	6. True
1. B	7. B	2. B	7. True
2. A	8. B	3. A	8. False – they can pop only as high as 0.9m (3ft) in the air.
3. B	9. A	4. B	
4. C	10. C	5. C	9. False
5. B	11. C	6. C	10. True
	12. B		
Page 63	13. C		
1. B	14. C		
2. B	15. C		

Acknowledgments

The publisher would like to thank the following for their kind permission to reproduce their photographs:

(Key: a-above; b-below/bottom; c-centre; f-far; l-left; r-right; t-top)

10 **Fotosearch:** Image Zoo Illustrations (bl, br, fbr). 11 **Dorling Kindersley:** Peter Hayman / The Trustees of the British Museum (bl). 13 **Dorling Kindersley:** James Stevenson / The National Maritime Museum, London (ftr). 18 **Dorling Kindersley:** Clive Streeter / The Science Museum, London (crb); **Dreamstime.com:** Paulpaladin (cra). 21 **Dorling Kindersley:** Tim Parmenter / The Natural History Museum, London (crb, fcla). 23 **Science Photo Library:** R. Bick, B.

Poindexter, UT Medical School (clb); Nancy Kedersha / UCLA (cla); Steve Gschmeissner (cl). 25 **Dorling Kindersley:** Clive Streeter (cla); Gary Ombler (cla). 29 **Science Photo Library:** Herve Conge, ISM (tl); Steve Gschmeissner (bc). 33 **Dreamstime.com:** Paulpaladin (clb, tr, fbr, clb, cla, clb). 36 **Photolibrary:** FoodCollection (ftr). 38 **Dreamstime.com:** Ljupco Smokovski / Ljupco (bl, br). 39 **Dreamstime.com:** Ljupco Smokovski / Ljupco (bl, br, tr). 40 **Fotolia:** Ruth Black (cla). 44 **Photolibrary:** FoodCollection (clb). 45 **Fotolia:** Ruth Black (clb, gbl). 49 **Dreamstime.com:** Andrey Sukhachev / Nchuprin (ftl). 87 **Dorling Kindersley:** Frank Greenaway / The Natural History Museum, London (ca, cra, fbl).

All other images © Dorling Kindersley For further information see: www.dkimages.com

DK would also like to thank Marie Lorimer for preparing the index, and Lee Wilson for proofreading.